The Concept of P

The Concept of Presocratic Philosophy

ITS ORIGIN, DEVELOPMENT, AND SIGNIFICANCE

André Laks

Translated by Glenn W. Most

PRINCETON & OXFORD

Princeton University Press

First paperback printing, 2019
Paperback ISBN 9780691191485

The Library of Congress has cataloged the cloth edition as follows:

Names: Laks, André, author.
Title: The concept of presocratic philosophy : its origin, development, and
    significance / André Laks ; translated by Glenn W. Most.
Other titles: Introduction à la philosophie présocratique. English
Description: Princeton : Princeton University Press, 2018. | Includes
    bibliographical references and index.
Identifiers: LCCN 2017014688 | ISBN 9780691175454 (hardcover : alk. paper)
Subjects: LCSH: Pre-Socratic philosophers.
Classification: LCC B187.5 .L3513 2018 | DDC 182—dc23
    LC record available at https://lccn.loc.gov/2017014688

British Library Cataloging-in-Publication Data is available
This book has been composed in Adobe Jensen Pro
Printed on acid-free paper. ∞
Printed in the United States of America

N. A. T.

CONTENTS

PREFACE

THE ORIGINAL FRENCH VERSION OF THIS BOOK WAS PUBLISHED in 2004 under the title *Introduction à la "philosophie présocratique."* I have modified the text only slightly, essentially doing so only to eliminate certain mistakes or infelicitous phrases and to update the references. As its title indicates, the purpose of this essay is to explain the intellectual circumstances that led to a loose group of early Greek thinkers being considered collectively under the designation of "Presocratic philosophers," and, even more concisely, under that of just "Presocratics." Those thinkers whom we call the Presocratics did not conceive of themselves as being Presocratics, for a reason even more radical than the one for which the Neoplatonists did not consider themselves to be Neoplatonists: Socrates was not a reference point for them. At most, he was their contemporary—indeed, in some cases, a somewhat younger contemporary. And again it is at most only quite late, at the end of the period that is included under the designation of "Presocratic philosophy," that these thinkers began to be called "philosophers." But if it is only retroactively that the Presocratic philosophers are philosophers and Presocratics, then it is worth asking how they became "Presocratic philosophers"— in order to cast light upon this construction, to be sure, but also in order to ask to what degree it is legitimate. This latter question explains why I prefer not to use the term "invention," which too readily suggests arbitrariness.

The importance of this semantic approach is evidently connected with the fact that when we speak of the Presocratic philosophers, what we are speaking about is the origins of Greek philosophy, and hence also about the origins of Western rationality. This explains the organization of this book. It starts out with typological questions connected with the use of the phrase "Presocratic philosophy" in Antiquity (chapter 1) and in the modern period (chapter 2), disentangling the stakes that underlie this designation, in order to go on to discuss the meaning of "philosophy" in the present context (chapter 3), the question of "rationality" (chapter 4), and the very notion of "origin" (chapter 5). It concludes by comparing two philosophical models of the historiography of philosophy, deriving in the one case from the phenomenological tradition, in the other from a rationalist one, represented respectively and paradigmatically by Gadamer, on the one hand, and Cassirer, on the other (chapter 6). Even though my own preference tends clearly toward the latter model, I am not proposing here any approach that could be immune to the criticisms that can be addressed to either one of them, whether regarding their general orientation or particular applications.

References to the fragments of the Presocratic authors are made, whenever possible, both to the edition of reference (Hermann Diels and Walter Kranz, *Die Fragmente der Vorsokratiker*, 6th edition, Berlin, 1951–52, indicated as DK) and to the edition recently coedited by Glenn W. Most and myself (André Laks and Glenn W. Most, *Early Greek Philosophy*, Loeb Classical Library, 9 volumes, Cambridge, MA, 2016, indicated as LM). The full references for works and studies, which are cited in the notes by the name of the author followed by the date of the publication used, will be found in the bibliography; the second date that sometimes appears between parentheses refers to the date of the original publication. The translations of the Greek texts cited were either derived from the Loeb edition that Glenn W. Most and I have published (as above) or made by Glenn; he is also responsible for all translations from modern European languages unless these are otherwise attributed.

Glenn first suggested to me that an English translation of this small book would be useful, all the more as it refers more often to the so-called Continental tradition than the Anglo-Saxon one, and he spontaneously offered to translate it. I thank him very much for his initiative. I also wish to thank the readers of Princeton University Press and Ben Tate, the editor responsible for this subject area, who have made this publication possible.

The Concept of Presocratic Philosophy

~

CHAPTER 1

Presocratics: Ancient Antecedents

THE TERM "PRESOCRATIC" IS A MODERN CREATION. THE EARLIest attestation discovered so far is found in a manual of the universal history of philosophy published in 1788 by J.-A. Eberhard (the addressee of a famous letter by Kant): one section is entitled "Presocratic Philosophy" ("*vorsokratische Philosophie*").[1] But the idea that there is a major caesura between Socrates and what preceded him goes back to Antiquity. In order to understand the modern debates that have developed around the Presocratics, it is indispensable to go back to these ancient Presocratics, whom by convention I propose to designate "pre-Socratics" (in lowercase, and with a hyphen), in order to distinguish them from the "Presocratics," the historiographical category to whose creation they contributed but under which they cannot be entirely subsumed. Even if undeniable similarities make the ancient "pre-Socratics" the natural ancestors of our modern Presocratics, the differences between the two groups are in fact not less significant, in particular with regard to the stakes involved in both of them.

Antiquity knew of two ways to conceive of the dividing line between what preceded Socrates and what followed him: either Socrates abandoned a philosophy of *nature* for the sake of a philosophy of *man* (this is the perspective that I shall call Socratic-Ciceronian, which also includes Xenophon), or he passed from a philosophy of *things* to a philosophy of the *concept* (this is the Platonic-Aristotelian tradition). Although a bridge was constructed between these two traditions, notably by Plato in the *Phaedo* (a text that is both complex and decisive for the posterity of the Presocratics), they diverge not only in their tenor but also, and even more, in their effects: while the former only thematizes a certain rupture, the latter by contrast brings to light the thread of a deeper continuity beyond it. This dissymmetry, which can be, and indeed has been, specified in different ways, is essential for understanding the modern fate of the Presocratics. It is worth examining precisely its presuppositions and its consequences.

At its origin, the Socratic-Ciceronian tradition is closely connected with Socrates's trial (399 BCE), in which, in order to respond to the accusation of impiety with which (among other things) he was charged, he needed to distinguish himself from an enterprise that had been known at least since the 430s under the name of "inquiry into nature" (*peri phuseôs historia*).

The *Phaedo* strongly suggests that the phrase "inquiry into nature" was still perceived as a technical expression at the dramatic date of the conversation it portrays (which is supposed to have occurred on the very day of Socrates's death), and we cannot exclude the possibility that this was still the case at the date of the composition of the dialogue, about fifteen years later. For the Socrates of the *Phaedo* says that when he was young he "was incredibly eager for the kind of wisdom *that is called* the inquiry into nature," which he expected would give him the knowledge of "the causes of each thing, why each thing comes into being and why it perishes and why it exists."[2] The specification "that is called" points to the novelty of the expression, if not to that of the enterprise itself.

In fact, none of the surviving texts that refer to such an "inquiry into nature" is older than the last third of the fifth century BCE. It is also around this time—and evidently not by chance—that the title "On Nature" comes into circulation, and that it is applied, in certain cases anachronistically, to older works that fell (or were thought to fall) within this genre.[3]

In chapter 20 of the Hippocratic treatise *On Ancient Medicine* (which also happens to present the first-known occurrence of the abstract term *philosophia*[4]), its author, a medical writer who advocates traditional methods, distances himself from writings "on nature" that he judges to be too speculative because of the presuppositions (or "hypotheses") they are led to adopt, and contrasts them with medical inquiry as the sole legitimate source of knowledge about the nature of man:[5]

> But what they are talking about belongs to philosophy, like Empedocles or others who have written about nature: what a human being is from the beginning, how he first appeared and out of what things he is constituted. But as for me, I think that whatever has been said or written by some expert [*sophistês*] or doctor about nature belongs less to the art of medicine than to that of painting,[6] and I think that there is no other source than medicine for having some clear knowledge about nature.... I say that this field of inquiry [*tautên tên historiên*] knows exactly what a human being is, through what causes he comes about, and everything else.[7]

The second passage is a fragment of Euripides that scholars tend to attribute to a lost tragedy, *Antiope*, which is known to have contained a debate, famous in Antiquity, between the two brothers Amphion and Zethus regarding the utility and the value of music, and by extension that of intellectual studies:

> [Chorus:] Happy the man who, having attained
> The *knowledge deriving from inquiry* [*tês historias ... mathêsin*],
> Aspires neither to trouble for his fellow citizens
> Nor to unjust deeds,
> *But observes immortal nature's*
> *Unaging order, where it was formed,*
> *In what way, and how.*
> Never to men like this does the practice
>   of shameful actions come near.[8]

The third passage comes from an anonymous dialectical set of arguments known under the title of *Dissoi Logoi* (Pairs of arguments):

> I think that it belongs to the same man and to the same art to be able to discuss briefly, to know the truth of things, to judge a legal case correctly, to be able to make speeches to the people, to know the arts of speeches, and *to teach about the nature of all things, both their present condition and their origins.*[9]

On the basis of these three texts, which echo the passage from the *Phaedo* and each other, we can see that "the inquiry into nature" involved two principal characteristics. On the one hand, it is directed toward a totality (it bears upon "all things" or upon "the whole"). On the other hand, it adopts a resolutely genetic perspective (it explains the existing condition of things by tracing the history of its development from the *origins*).

One can identify fairly well the stages that, after a process of rapid crystallization, ended up transforming the authors of treatises on "the nature of all things" into "natural philosophers," those thinkers whom Aristotle called simply "naturalists" (*phusikoi*).[10] In a passage of the *Memorabilia* that echoes the one in the *Phaedo*, Xenophon still has recourse to a comprehensive expression when, in the context of a defense of Socrates to which we shall return in a moment, he maintains that "he never discoursed, like most of the others, *about the nature of all things* [*peri tês tôn pantôn phuseôs*], investigating the condition of what the experts call 'the world order' [*hopôs ho kaloumenos hupo tôn sophistôn kosmos ekhei*] and by what necessities each of the heavenly phenomena occurs."[11] Plato's *Lysis* mentions the "totality" (named by the other term, *holon*, which Greek can use to designate a totality of things), but dissociates it from "nature": the sages, who, together with Homer, maintain "that like must always be friend to like," are presented as "speaking and writing on nature and on the whole" (*hoi peri phuseôs te kai tou holou dialegomenoi kai graphontes*).[12] But after the *Phaedo*, the term "nature" can come to stand in for whole expression. Thus Socrates asks in the *Philebus*, "And if someone supposes that he is conducting research on nature [*peri phuseôs ... zêtein*], do you know that he does research for his whole life on what has to do with this world, how it has come about, how it is affected, and how it acts [*ta peri ton kosmon tonde, hopê te gegonen kai hopê paskhei kai hopê poiei*]?"[13] This substitution of the term "nature" for the more detailed expression leads to the threshold of the substantivizations of Aristotle, who employs very frequently, and as synonyms, "the authors (of treatises) on nature" (*hoi peri phuseôs*), "the naturalists" (*hoi phusikoi*), or sometimes "the physiologues" (*hoi phusiologoi*).[14]

In fact, there is a lineage of works among the Presocratic thinkers that corresponds to this description, of which the basic scheme
very probably goes back to Anaximander.[15] What is involved is a
general history of the universe and of its constitutive parts, from its
beginnings until a limit that seems most often to have gone beyond
the current condition of the world and to have been constituted by
the moment of its destruction (thus it would be more exact to speak
of "cosmo-gono-phthorias" than of simple cosmogonies). The narrative comprised a certain number of elements that were more or
less obligatory. From Anaximander to Philolaus and Democritus,
by way of Anaximenes, Parmenides (in the second part of his poem),
Empedocles, Anaxagoras, Diogenes of Apollonia, and others of
lesser importance, the grand narratives "on nature" include an explanation of the way in which the universe, the heavenly bodies, and
the earth were formed, with, already very early, discussion of more
technical or specialized problems like the delimitation of the celestial and terrestrial zones, the inclination of the poles, the distance
and size of the heavenly bodies, the luminosity of the moon, meteorological and terrestrial phenomena, rain and hail, earthquakes
and tides, the origin of living beings and their reproduction, the
sexual differentiation of embryos, the mechanism of physiological
life, sleep and death, sensation and thought, and in some cases the
development of life in society. In short: a cosmogony and a cosmology, a zoogony and a zoology, an anthropology and a physiology (in
the modern sense of the term), which under certain circumstances
could also be continued as a history of human civilization.[16]

Out of this complex whole, certain ancient texts retain essentially the cosmological aspect, and speak of "meteorology" and of
"meteorologists": for before the Aristotelian distinction between a
supralunary region and an infralunary one, which tends to limit *meteôra* to the domain of "meteorological" phenomena alone, the term
meteôra designated any phenomena occurring "on high," and represented by synecdoche the whole of the inquiry into nature. In the
opening scene of the *Protagoras*, the audience asks the sophist Hippias "a number of astronomical questions about nature and celestial
phenomena [*meteôra*]."[17] And it is only by contrast with "celestial

phenomena" that the author of the Hippocratic treatise *Fleshes* (who is opposed on this point to the author of *On Ancient Medicine*) delimited the field of medicine from the naturalists' research:

> I need say nothing about celestial phenomena [*peri tôn meteôrôn*] except insofar as I shall indicate their relevance to humans and the other animals—how they are born by nature and came to exist, what the soul is, what it is to be healthy, what it is to be sick, what is bad and good in the human, and whence it comes that he dies.[18]

But it is clear that the series of questions that Socrates enumerates in the *Phaedo* as having attracted the passion of his younger years also derives from the subjects the naturalists discussed within the framework of a totalizing program:

> Are living creatures nourished when heat and cold undergo a kind of putrefaction, as some people say? Is it rather blood by which we think, or air, or fire? Or is it none of these, but rather the brain that supplies the sensations of hearing, sight, and smell, and from these latter that memory and opinion arise, and, when memory and opinion achieve a state of stability, does knowledge come about in accordance with these? And again, investigating the perishing of these processes, I also investigated what happens in the heavens and on earth.[19]

It is significant that the subjects mentioned by Socrates concern especially the physiology of knowledge, as though from the beginning Socrates had been more interested in questions that had, at least virtually, an epistemological scope than in accounts of the structure of the universe. Naturalism, born in Ionia, and in particular in Miletus, in the sixth century BCE, had been introduced into Athens by Anaxagoras, whom Pericles invited in 456/55 to become part of his entourage.[20] There it rapidly became an object of suspicion. The general tone is indicated by another fragment of Euripides, from an unknown play, that takes a position opposed to the praise for the life of study pronounced by Amphion in the *Antiope*:

Who when he sees these things does not begin by teaching
His soul to conceive of god,
And *casts far away the crooked deceptions of those who study the
heavens,*
Whose audacious tongue guesses at random about invisible
matters
without having any share in judgment?[21]

The debate regarding the harmlessness or harmfulness of meteorology was not at all merely theoretical. The decree of Diopeithes,
which permitted those who busied themselves with matters "on high"
to be prosecuted under the charge of impiety, dates from 438/37.
In the following year, its first victim was Anaxagoras (through
whom Pericles was the intended target), for having maintained that
the heavenly bodies were nothing but burning stones. Diogenes of
Apollonia may also have been formally accused, several years after
Anaxagoras, although this is disputed.[22] Strange as it might seem,
given that this tallies so badly with the image we have of Socrates
on the basis of Plato's *Apology of Socrates* and Xenophon's *Memorabilia*, Socrates was suspected of sharing the naturalists' curiosity
about the mechanisms of the universe and consequently their impiety. The key document in this connection is constituted by Aristophanes's *Clouds*, staged in 423 BCE, which the *Apology of Socrates* denounces explicitly as the first real attack on Socrates, about
twenty-five years before his trial in 399.[23]

In fact, the *Clouds*, in anticipating the two accusations to which
Socrates had to reply—corrupting the youth and introducing gods
unknown to the city—displayed a Socrates who is indissociably
both a "sophist," someone capable of making "the weaker" argument
"the stronger" one, and at the same time a "natural philosopher," sus-
pended in a basket and propagating scraps extracted parodistically
from the doctrine of Diogenes of Apollonia, who maintained that
the air on high was endowed with an intelligence that was greater
because it was drier.[24]

The *Apology* denounces this amalgam[25] as the product of a pure
calumny: no one has ever heard Socrates discussing "what is below

the earth and in the sky."[26] Xenophon's *Memorabilia* repeats this: "No one ever saw Socrates doing, or heard him saying, anything impious or irreligious. For he never discoursed, like most of the others, about the nature of all things, investigating the condition of what the sophists call 'the world order' [*kosmos*] and by what necessities each of the heavenly phenomena occurs."[27] So far from meddling with "divine things," like the naturalists, Socrates directed his interest resolutely toward "human things" (*ta anthrôpina*), the good of man and the practice of virtue. Both in Xenophon and in Plato's *Apology*, Socrates becomes the figure of the first "humanist"—a humanism that is distinguished by its resolute rejection of all physical speculation. This is what is also meant, in a way that is at the same time more traditional and less transparent, by the well-attested formula according to which Socrates occupied himself not with physics but with ethics.[28]

The simple and rhetorically effective opposition between pre-Socratic "naturalism" and Socratic "humanism" was intended in the first instance to mark a typological difference between two kinds of intellectual orientation. But it also opened the way for a historiographical interpretation, in virtue of which one orientation *follows* the other. The *Phaedo*, which also develops a more complex image of the relation between Socrates and ancient physics than the one presented in the *Apology* or the *Memorabilia*, indisputably favored such an interpretation by recalling what the *Apology* and the *Memorabilia*, for understandable reasons, had taken great care not to mention: namely, that Socrates himself had gone through a naturalist phase in his earlier years. We have already encountered this passage: "When I myself was young, I was incredibly eager for the kind of wisdom that they call the investigation of nature. For it seemed to me splendid to know the causes of each thing, why each thing comes into being and why it perishes and why it exists."[29] The doxographic tradition provides more precise outlines for this statement when it makes Socrates the disciple of Archelaus, himself a natural philosopher located within Anaxagoras's sphere of influence but one who is said to have dealt with ethics too (this last feature was perhaps intended to facilitate the transition).[30]

Plato was perfectly capable of constructing a biographical fiction for the sake of the cause.[31] But the idea of a Socrates who was once an adept of natural philosophy is not devoid of plausibility, not only from an intrinsic point of view (one has to start somewhere), but also because it lets us understand how Aristophanes could have put into Socrates's mouth statements that were typical of natural philosophy, even if in 423 Socrates, by then forty-six years old, and already celebrated for being the person he really was, was certainly no longer speculating about meteorological or physiological phenomena. In any case, from the point of view of the historicization of the pre-Socratics, the important point is that if the Socrates of the *Phaedo* does not practice physical speculation, this is not only because it is alien to him, but also and especially because by now he has *separated* himself from it. The two epochs of the history of thought that future histories of philosophy will distinguish—before Socrates and after him—are in origin two epochs of the life of the one and only Socrates himself, who practiced natural philosophy before he became himself.

The quasi-historiographical use of the pre-Socratics, detached from biographical considerations, is fully attested for the first time in the prologue of the fifth book of Cicero's *Tusculan Disputations*, which by reason of its very large diffusion (and apparent simplicity) probably exerted the greatest influence on the constitution of the modern concept of the Presocratics.

This prologue contains a forceful encomium of philosophy as practical philosophy. Not only does philosophy assert that virtue is sufficient for happiness (a claim whose merits Cicero had every reason to appreciate in the particularly difficult situation in which he found himself while he was composing this work); it is also at the origin of all the benefits that humanity enjoys. For it is to philosophy that man is indebted for the formation of cities, with all the social, cultural, legal, and moral bonds that political life presupposes.[32] Only the uneducated do not know that "those by whom the life of men was first organized were philosophers."[33] In such a perspective, the history of philosophy is coextensive with the history of civilization.

Cicero distinguishes three stages. In the first, primitive phase of the development of societies, philosophers exist, but under a different name, that of "sages." These are not only the "Seven Sages," of which there existed a traditional and more-or-less established list,[34] but also mythical or quasi-mythical figures like Odysseus, Nestor, Atlas, Prometheus, Cepheus, or Lycurgus. It is to Pythagoras that the role is assigned of having been the first to introduce the term "philosophy," with which the wisdom of the sages takes a different turn. Pythagoras explains to the tyrant Leon, who is intrigued by this neologism, that unlike the sages, who are busy with their civilizing activity, the philosophers dedicate themselves to "theory," observing for the sake of observation, without being guided by any other motive than the contentment that this observation provides them. The analogy he offers is celebrated: just as an athletic competition brings together not only athletes struggling for glory, and merchants and customers attracted by the commerce, but also spectators who have come to admire the competition, so too there exist in this life not only ambitious people and merchants but also the small group of those people who, "counting everything else as nothing, carefully examine the nature of things": it is these, the pure "theoreticians," who are called "philosophers."[35] In Cicero's presentation of him, Pythagoras still combines within himself "wisdom" and "philosophy": no sooner has he given Leon the explanation mentioned above than he leaves to legislate in Magna Graecia. But by its nature, theoretical activity has a tendency to be exclusive. The philosophers who come after Pythagoras are no longer anything but pure theoreticians: henceforth they are remote from practical questions. It is to Socrates that the role will be assigned of having reintroduced these latter questions into the field of philosophy, which in this way he leads back (according to a celebrated phrase) "from the sky to the earth," where it had originally been rooted but which in the meantime it had abandoned.

Although Cicero does not hesitate to identify the totality of the postsapiential and pre-Socratic philosophers with meteorologists, indeed with astronomers, the periodization he adopts, once it was accepted, inevitably led to a reinterpretation of the concept of "nature." For although among the thinkers earlier than Socrates there were indeed many who correspond to the characteristics of the inquiry on nature, this is not the case for all of them. Neither Parmenides, nor (even less) his disciples Melissus and Zeno, nor Heraclitus is a naturalist in the sense described above: in different degrees and each in his own way, their aim is instead to mark the limits of such an inquiry, indeed to put its very legitimacy into question. But the concept of "nature" is complex enough that thinkers who did not belong at all, or did not do so essentially, to the "inquiry on nature" were capable of being considered to have been "natural philosophers." Xenophon already explains that one of the reasons for Socrates's hostility with regard to the "natural philosophers" had to do with the uncertainties to which the knowledge they claimed was subject, and to which the divergence of their position regarding the question of knowing *what the number of beings is* testifies.[36] Now, in a way that is surprising at first glance, not only are those people who practice the inquiry into nature considered to be "natural philosophers" here, but also those who deny the existence of any change, and thus that of the "natural" processes of generation and corruption (i.e., Parmenides and his Eleatic disciples). "*Among those who are preoccupied with the nature of all things,* some think that what is is only one, others that it is infinite in number; the ones that all things are always in motion, *the others that nothing could ever be in motion*; and the ones that all things come into being and are destroyed, *the others that nothing could ever either come into being or be destroyed.*"[37]

For the Eleatics to be capable of being understood as "natural philosophers," the meaning of the term "nature" cannot be exactly identical with that in the *Phaedo*. It is easy to reconstruct the logic of the slippage that produces the transition from a narrow sense to a more general one. "Nature" (*phusis*) can refer in Greek not only to the processes of genesis and corruption, that is, to the visible or official aspect of the inquiry into nature, but also to the "nature" that is deployed and subsists through these processes—what Aristotle will call the "principle" (*arkhê*) or "substrate" (*hupokeimenon*), "of which all beings are made, that from which they arise at the beginning and into which they return at the end."[38] Then it is enough to interpret the originary "nature" ontologically, recognizing it as "what truly is" (by opposition to the things or composites that have arisen from it), for the study of nature to be capable of including even the thesis of those who refuse to attribute all the determinations of "nature" in a more restricted sense to "what is," that is, to "nature" in the broad sense. It is precisely this ontological conception of nature that Xenophon, or his source, puts at the basis of the debate among the naturalists, because this latter bears not on the sky and natural phenomena, but on the number and quality of *beings*. It is in this way that the pre-Socratics are also the first ontologists.[39]

Antiquity never officially adopted the classification that has been sketched out here: as a general rule, the naturalists remained naturalists *stricto sensu*, even if ancient tradition reports that Parmenides's writings, and even more Melissus's, were entitled "On Nature," like those of the "natural philosophers."[40] Although Aristotle employed a concept of nature that was sufficiently differentiated to justify the transition from one sense of *phusis* to the other, he always respects the distinction between the majority of the ancient philosophers, constituted by the "natural philosophers," and the others, who refuse nature (the Eleatics in general) or who only accept it as a kind of second best (Parmenides). Aristotle's need to assign clear limits to physics from his own point of view, by distinguishing it not only from dialectic and mathematics but also from first philosophy, impelled him to maintain the demarcation, even if he does not coin a general designation for the second group. Only the Skeptic Sextus Empiricus, in a passage that refers to the Aristotelian demarcation, assigns the Eleatics the names of "immobilists" (*stasiôtai*) and "non-naturalists" (*aphusikoi*).[41]

The Socratic-Ciceronian tradition is characterized by the fact that it locates the rupture between Socrates and his predecessors at the level of a certain *content*, in certain cases linked to a definite epistemological attitude: before Socrates, nature, the sky, and more generally being, within a purely theoretical perspective; starting with Socrates, man, his action, and morality, within the perspective of an essentially practical philosophy. The Platonic-Aristotelian tradition, by contrast, locates this rupture at the level of the *method*, that is, of the instruments that allow the contents to become objects of thought: one might say that it attributes to Socrates a second-order

kind of thought, by opposition to the first-order kind that was characteristic of his predecessors.[42] This shift toward epistemological
questions, which evidently can open up the possibility of reinter-
preting not only Socrates himself but also the pre-Socratics, occurs
for the first time in the *Phaedo* of Plato. Just as Plato sketches out,
by means of the theory of contraries and of the formal cause, the
categories that direct Aristotle's physics as it is developed in the first
book of his *Physics*, so too does he pave the way for the essentially
continuist history of the beginnings of philosophy that Aristotle
will narrate in the first book of his *Metaphysics*. It is all as though,
at the end of a process that has now been concluded, and at the very
moment that Socrates is about to be executed (as I recalled earlier,
the *Phaedo* takes place on this very day), it at last becomes possible
to deploy a more philosophically balanced vision than the one that
was allowed by the needs of his defense.

In the story that Socrates tells about his own intellectual development, which constitutes a long digression within the last of his
arguments in favor of the immortality of the soul, he recalls the
circumstances that led him to undertake a "second sailing" (*deuteros
plous*), once he had recognized the aporias of the physics that had at
first aroused his passions and its inability to give an account of the
final cause. This time, the rupture, deep though it is, occurs only on
the basis of a shared philosophical project, as is suggested by the very
metaphor of the second sailing, which presupposes that one and the
same voyage is being continued, even if by other means.[43]

Cebes has just formulated an objection against Socrates's last
argument: to establish that the soul pre-exists our birth, Cebes remarks, does not in the least allow us to conclude that it is immortal.[44] For it is quite possible that, even if the soul did pre-exist, it
could be corruptible in the end, and that its entrance into a body
marked the beginning of a process of deterioration that will lead
ineluctably to its destruction, and that this would be the case even
if one had to agree that it would last for a certain time.

To answer this objection, Socrates acknowledges, is no light task.
This presupposes "a profound investigation into the cause of generation and corruption in general." However, the "inquiry into nature,"
which is supposed to deal with this topic (it discusses "what comes

about and what is destroyed"[45]), is not up to this task. So far from
rendering explicit the cause (*aition*) of the processes of generation
and corruption, it only talks about the material conditions that are
necessary for their effectuation, what Plato in the *Timaeus* calls by
the technical term of the "auxiliary causes" (*sunaitia*).[46] Indeed, only
the cause that Aristotle will call "that for the sake of which" (the
final cause) corresponds to what Socrates understands here under
the name of cause. That is why, for a moment, he had placed his
hopes in Anaxagoras, who was the only natural philosopher, according to the text of the *Phaedo*, to detach himself from the anonymous mass of his peers by maintaining that "intelligence organized
the world and is the cause of all things."[47] The problem is that this
statement in Anaxagoras, according to Socrates's reading of it, is not
followed by any effect, given that he explains the formation of the
world by what Socrates, using a pejorative plural, calls "airs, aethers,
waters, and many other strange entities."[48]

However, the second sailing, directed "toward the search for
causes,"[49] does not lead directly all the way to the final cause. It bor-
rows the path of a hypothetical procedure resting on a theory of the
formal cause (the Forms as causes). The argument by which Socrates will establish the incorruptibility of the soul in order to respond
finally to Cebes consists in saying that neither a Form itself, like
Cold, nor any entity depending upon the presence of such a Form,
like snow, would be capable of receiving within itself a contrary Form
(in the present case, Heat). Either one or the other of two things
must happen: they will have to "either perish or withdraw"—perish,
if the entity in question is perishable, like snow; withdraw, if the
entity in question is exempt from death by essence or definition.
But this last hypothesis applies to life, of which the concept, according to Socrates, analytically implies "immortality." The soul too,
which is its principle, will be immortal, and hence "incorruptible."

This argument, which could be called "biological" (as one speaks
of the "ontological argument"), invokes an example belonging to
"ethics" at one of its stages: if Socrates remains in prison, this is not
because of his bones and muscles, which are only necessary conditions, but because he thinks this is right.[50] The use of these distinc-
tively Platonic philosophemes makes the transition from the pre-

Socratics to Socrates coincide with the one from a purely Socratic Socrates to a distinctly Platonic Socrates.[51] But the main argument, to which this example is subordinated, does not bear upon human affairs. Instead it sketches the outlines of a new physics, of which the distinctive mark would be that it is structured teleologically.[52] Thus at the horizon of the "second sailing" of the *Phaedo* we glimpse the *Timaeus*, which, in renewing a connection with the "naturalists'" cosmological project, constitutes a decisive moment in the reappropriation of the Socrates of the *Apology* by the science of natural phenomena. Suggestive evidence is provided by the final eschatological myth of the *Phaedo*, with the geographic-cosmological description of the world where the souls are divided up after death, including a hydrology that Aristotle criticizes in his *Meteorologica* as Plato's theory "on rivers and the sea."[53]

Aristotle did not follow Plato on this path, which indubitably effaces what was distinctive about Socrates for the sake of a problematic that is no longer Socrates's own. But nonetheless Aristotle takes over the idea that the pre-Socratics and Socrates are engaged in the same enterprise, of which the object is not what comes to be and what perishes, but more generally the search for causes. It is precisely this that earns them the name of "first philosophers," or more exactly that of "the first ones to philosophize," which Aristotle awards them in the first book of the *Metaphysics*.[54]

Starting with chapter 3, *Metaphysics* 1, which opens with a characterization of the highest knowledge as "wisdom," is dedicated to discovering among Aristotle's predecessors ("the first philosophers," but also Socrates and Plato) the emergence of the four causes, for which the *Physics* had presented the systematic table: first, the material cause, of which Aristotle wonders whether or not one can already attribute the notion to the poets and to the group of those whom he designates as "the theologians" (the authors of theogonies, like Hesiod or the Orphics) rather than to Thales; then, in order, the efficient cause, about which one might "suspect" that Hesiod had a notion even before Parmenides; the final cause, in Anaxagoras and Empedocles (chapters 3 and 4); and the formal cause among the Pythagoreans and Plato (chapters 5 and 6). Given that these are the "first philosophers," what is involved is not so much discoveries as rather anticipations. The final cause, in Empedocles, is called "Friend-ship" or "Love" (*Philia*); in Anaxagoras, it is implied by the directive function of the mind; the efficient cause, again, is called "Love" (*Eros*) in Hesiod and Parmenides. And the "bodies" themselves that the naturalists take as principles are nothing but the prefiguration of the substrate and of potentiality. In such a perspective, there is an unbroken continuity from Thales to Plato.[55] Although he mentions that Socrates "busied himself with ethical matters and not with na-ture as a whole,"[56] Aristotle, far from locating his contribution to the history of philosophy in this very choice, suggests instead its contin-gent character: what Socrates was the first to do, "seeking with re-gard to them [i.e., ethical questions] the universal," was to interest himself in definitions.[57] This novelty is itself conceived as the prem-ise for the Platonic theory of the Forms, the last theory of principles to be presented by Aristotle before the recapitulation in chapter 7, the criticism in chapters 8 and 9, and the conclusion in chapter 10, which confers upon Socrates a status of an intermediary rather than one of an initiator.

This interpretation of Socrates is found again in the parallel passage of Book 13 of the *Metaphysics* (except that there Aristotle specifies the contribution of Democritus and, earlier, of the Pythag-oreans with regard to the search for definitions[58]), and it is also de-ployed in the first book of the *Parts of Animals*.[59] The question is that of the method in biology. Pointing ironically, though implicitly, to the distance that separates the "natural philosophers'" preten-tions from their accomplishments, Aristotle defends the idea that there exist two sorts of causes of which the naturalist must take account on pain of missing "nature": the final cause (which in this context includes the formal cause) and necessity (which belongs to "matter").[60] Aristotle explains that the reason why his predecessors were never able to envisage the final cause except by a lucky chance (they do nothing more than "stumble upon" it) is that the practice of the definition of essence had still been foreign to them: even Dem-ocritus, of whom it was true that he engaged himself in the search for definitions, does it because "he was guided by the thing itself" (in an unreflective way), and not "because it would be necessary for physics" (in a conscious way). Socrates, for his part, did indeed contribute to the progress of the theory of definition, but since he followed the inclination, common to the philosophers of his era, "toward useful virtue and politics," he provided no benefit to physics. From this point of view, Aristotelian physics—which gives a place to the final (and formal) cause next to the material cause, thanks to an explicit theory of definition and of essence—can be seen as a synthesis of the older Presocratic physics and of a Socratic impulse that turns out to be of an essentially epistemological nature.

Thus the image that emerges from Aristotle is complex. On the one hand, there does indeed exist a sequence passing from physics to ethics (and politics). But the attention directed to practice does not so much open a new era of philosophy as it characterizes the interest and spirit of a generation (the expression "the philosophers," *hoi philosophountes*, in the plural, might even include the "sophists"). Even though Socrates himself has a share in this common interest, ethics is scarcely more than the domain or the material to which he applies a different kind of concern. Socrates, a philosopher of definition, is inscribed within the continuity of a tradition that he contributes to regenerating rather than concluding. In such a perspective, the Socratic caesura is at the same time maintained and subordinated.

Within ancient philosophical historiography, doubtless no manifestation of this relativization is more tangible than the place assigned to Socrates in Diogenes Laertius's *Lives and Opinions of Eminent Philosophers*. The very fact that Diogenes Laertius divides the whole of Greek philosophy into two lineages—the "Ionic" lineage, which he derives from Anaximander (and Thales), and an "Italic" lineage, at the beginning of which stands Pythagoras (and Pherecydes of Syros)—precluded any division of a Ciceronian type, which presupposes a unilinear development of the history of philosophy.[61] But in the very midst of the Ionic lineage, Socrates plays the role of an intermediary link between Archelaus, on the one hand, and Plato and the other Socratics on the other.[62]

Thus a major discontinuity in the history of philosophy tended to be reabsorbed by the introduction of a middle term: as we saw above,[63] the doxographical testimonia on Archelaus suggest that if he was elevated to the dignity of having been Socrates's teacher, this was less because it was he in particular who was lurking behind the anonymous "natural philosophers" of the *Phaedo* than because, fully devoted to the study of "nature" though he still was, he had already discussed ethical questions, even before Socrates appeared on the scene. It is not that Diogenes Laertius knew nothing of the Socratic rupture. Returning to the relation between Archelaus and Socrates when he enumerates the parts of philosophy (physics, ethics, and dialectic), he notes—copies out—that "until Archelaus, there was the natural variety [scil. of philosophy]; starting with Socrates, there was, as has been said, the ethical variety."[64] The chapter dedicated to Archelaus repeats this.[65] Nonetheless, it remains true that the occasional thematization of the Socratic rupture appears necessarily like a subordinate moment because of the construction of the whole. Not only are there no Presocratics in Diogenes Laertius: the pre-Socratics themselves do not enjoy anything more than a virtual existence there. From this point of view, the emergence in Eberhard of the formula "Presocratic philosophy"[66] confirms the fact, which is well attested otherwise, that the modern historiography of ancient philosophy was originally constructed against the schemes that had been inherited from Diogenes Laertius; needless to say, the Ciceronian model played a decisive role in this reconfiguration.

~

CHAPTER 2

Presocratics: The Modern Constellation

THE NEOLOGISM "PRESOCRATIC" APPEARED AT THE END OF THE eighteenth century and inaugurated a debate until it was finally adopted, not before the end of the following century. The conjunction of two factors permitted its eventual adoption: on the one hand, Nietzsche's philosophical re-evaluation of the Presocratics, and on the other, the editorial undertaking of H. Diels, the founder of modern studies on the Presocratics, who was to publish the first scientific edition of the relevant corpus of texts in 1903 under the title *Die Fragmente der Vorsokratiker—The Fragments of the Presocratics*.[1] Even so, the difficulties to which this expression is exposed have remained, and this explains why scholars have regularly proposed replacing it with other ones, considered less fraught or more adequate, among which Aristotle's "first philosophers"[2] is conspicuous. The history of the Presocratics is closely enough connected with that of their designation for it to be worth pausing to consider this.

The first difficulty of the term "Presocratic" has to do with the use it makes of Socrates's name. Eberhard's manual testifies immediately to this difficulty, since the period he called "Socratic" opens in fact with a series of paragraphs dedicated not to Socrates himself but to the Sophists. For the Sophists are not less interested in "man" than Socrates is. This is why W. T. Krug, in a history of ancient philosophy published in 1815, preferred to reserve for Plato the privilege of beginning a second period of the history of philosophy, assigning the Sophists and Socrates to the end of the preceding period.[3] How, then, could Socrates be claimed to constitute a turning point? It is against the devaluation of Socrates implied by this re-arrangement that Schleiermacher reacted in a communication he

delivered in the course of this same year of 1815 before the Berlin
Academy under the significant title "On the Value of Socrates as a
Philosopher."[4] Schleiermacher wonders about the "contradiction"
between the function that is traditionally assigned to Socrates, that
of opening a new philosophical era, and the characterization that is
given of his doctrine. If Socrates's only merit had been to have "led
back philosophy from the sky to the earth," according to Cicero's
formula,[5] then he would be nothing more than a representative of
that "common sense" which the popular philosophy of the eighteenth century had in fact tended to see in him, but to which Schleiermacher refuses to grant the slightest philosophical character.[6] In
order for Socrates to be able to remain "a major caesura of Hellenic
philosophy" (and Schleiermacher thinks that there are good reasons for him to remain this), he must be granted "a more philosophical kind of thought than is habitually the case."[7] Schleiermacher
locates this philosophical insight not in the introduction of a new
discipline, be it ethics, of which he notes emphatically that it pre-
existed Socrates (notably among the Pythagoreans), or dialectic
(already practiced by the Eleatics), but in the discovery of the "inter-
penetration of the three disciplines" (dialectic, ethics, and physics)
founded upon "the Idea of knowledge in itself"—nothing less than
the very idea of philosophy, according to Schleiermacher's systematic idea of it.[8]

Closer to Eberhard's conception (if not to his terminology) is
the articulation that Hegel adopts in his *Lectures on the History of
Philosophy*. Guided by the dialectic of object and subject, Hegel is
in effect led once again to relativize Socrates's role. If the criterion
for establishing the limit of a first period of Greek philosophy resides in abandoning an objective philosophy of nature, it is to the
Sophists that the role of initiating the following period is assigned,
insofar as they are the first representatives of the principle of subjectivity in the history of philosophy.[9] Against this resurgence of the
Sophists, Zeller restores to Socrates the role of a pivot in his *History of Greek Philosophy in Its Historical Development* (*Die Philosophie der Griechen in ihrer geschichtlichen Entwicklung*), of which the
first edition appears between 1844 and 1852.[10] His argumentation,
though it recalls Schleiermacher's, is closer to the ancient sources,

notably the Aristotelian ones. For if Socrates changes the aspect of philosophy, this is for Zeller above all because he is the first representative of a philosophy of the concept (*eidos*). As for the Sophists, they can perfectly well be counted among the Presocratics. For what they evince is the dissolution of a kind of philosophy, rather than a truly new philosophy.[11]

Zeller's periodization imposed itself as being at one and the same time the most plausible and the easiest one to use. It is upon this periodization that Diels's collection of the *Fragmente der Vorsokratiker*, first published in 1903, rests: it includes, next to the "natural philosophers" (understood in the broadest possible extension of this term), all the representatives of the Sophistic movement.[12] To this extent, Zeller and Diels are just as much "inventors of the Presocratics" as is Nietzsche, to whom this title has been attributed because of the decisive role he played in the extraordinary philosophical and intellectual prominence they enjoyed in the twentieth century.[13]

It is true that for a while Nietzsche, in the tradition of Krug (and Karsten), preferred to speak of "Preplatonics," or, more exactly, according to the title of the lectures he delivered at Basel probably starting in 1869, of "Preplatonic philosophers."[14] Here the line of demarcation passes between two types of philosophers, the ones, up to and including Socrates, being characterized, according to a new criterion of demarcation, by the originality and "purity" of their project, immune to the logic of compromise, and the others, starting with Plato, by the "hybrid" and dialectical (which for Nietzsche also means democratic) character of their philosophy.[15] It was only when the construction that made Socrates the first culprit of optimistic modernity came to dominate Nietzsche's mind in the years 1875/76 that Socrates become once again the true line of division, by the same token assuring for the Presocratics (hencefore considered as the only authentic "tyrants of the spirit") an advantage they were never again to be denied.[16]

Whether what is involved are Preplatonics or Presocratics, Nietzsche's interpretation performs a reversal with regard to the Ciceronian version of the pre-Socratics understood as "theoreticians." It is not that the first philosophers did not develop theories, and especially theories of nature. Nietzsche inclines all the less to deny this since, being a devoted reader of F. Lange's *History of Materialism* and of the works of the physicist Roger J. Boscovich, he sees among most of the Preplatonic philosophers potential allies in the combat waged by modern science against teleological thinking of every kind. Schopenhauer had already read Anaximenes, Empedocles, and Democritus in light of Kant and Laplace's cosmogony (did not Anaximenes also postulate the condensation of a diffuse matter, while Empedocles and Democritus posited a vortex?), and had identified the Pythagorean philosophy of numbers as a first form of "chemical stoichiometry" (i.e., the study of the quantitative parameters at work in chemical combinations),[17] without even mentioning the enthusiasm that Empedocles's thought inevitably aroused in this philosopher of pessimism ("he fully recognized the misery of our existence"[18]). Amplifying these remarks (and sometimes correcting them in doing so), Nietzsche insists on the fact that the Greek philosophers developed intuitions in which contemporary science can recognize itself. The lectures on the Preplatonic philosophers are regularly interrupted, each time the opportunity presents itself, by scientific excursuses—this is the case in the chapters devoted to Thales, Heraclitus, Empedocles, Democritus, and the Pythagoreans.[19]

The Kant-Laplace theory of the states of matter is invoked once again in order to explain the "water" that Thales made the origin of all things: "Actually, astronomical facts justify his belief that a less solid aggregate condition must have given rise to current circumstances." Heraclitus's "everything flows" is interpreted in the light of the concept of "force" (*Kraft*) developed by Helmholtz in his study "On the Reciprocal Action of the Forces of Nature": "Nowhere does an absolute persistence exist, because we always come in the final analysis to forces, whose effects simultaneously include a loss of power [*Kraftverlust*]." This interpretation permits a lengthy rapprochement with K. von Baer's biological relativism, which Nietzsche shares. As for Empedocles, he anticipates Darwin's biological evolutionism: the order of the world, so far from being the result of an intention (as in Anaxagoras), results from the blind interaction of two opposite impulses (*Triebe*).[20] "Obviously, in Empedocles we find kernels of a purely atomistic-materialistic viewpoint: the theory of chance forms—that is, all possible random combinations of elements, of which some are purposive and capable of life—belongs here with him"—a thought that Nietzsche calls "particularly brilliant." But the hero of the series is incontestably Democritus, the materialistic and anti-teleological philosopher. "Give me matter, and I will construct a world out of it."[21]

This Schopenhauerean-Nietzschean reading can seem not only naïve but also traditional, since, just as in Aristotle, the Preplatonic philosophers play the role of precursors. And yet it does innovate— with an innovation that not only justifies its naiveté, but in a certain way even calls for it. Not only does Nietzsche mobilize the science of the first philosophers against contemporary teleology, just as Schopenhauer had already done: he also refuses the teleological history-writing that turns each Preplatonic philosopher into a *stage* on the path of truth, as Aristotle had presented them in the first book of his *Metaphysics*. By putting *directly* into relation with one another Thales or Democritus and Kant/Laplace, Heraclitus and Helmholtz, Empedocles and Darwin, Nietzsche explodes the continuity of a progression in which each of the protagonists finds his meaning only by being surpassed. Perhaps the Preplatonic philosophers did produce anticipations: but by no means do they constitute merely provisional stages. The criterion of their greatness is not located beyond themselves. On the theoretical level, they are "great men," whose doctrines are interesting only insofar as they reveal a "personality."[22]

But Nietzsche's anti-Aristotelian (that is, antiteleological) line derives its meaning from a specific perspective whose framework is the modern problematic of the relation between the Ancients and the Moderns. Nietzsche's Preplatonic philosophers do not seek knowledge for the sake of knowledge; they are not practicing pure theory, as the image inherited from Antiquity suggested. On the contrary, they perform a corrective *function* within their own culture, which Nietzsche characterizes as fundamentally "tragic."[23]

The nature of Nietzsche's interest in the Preplatonic philosophers within the perspective of a philosophy of culture is made perfectly clear by the parallel that the fourth of his *Untimely Considerations* (*R. Wagner at Bayreuth*), dating from 1876, establishes between three representatives of that tragic culture (two philosophers and a dramatist) and three modern authors: Aeschylus, Parmenides, and Empedocles, on the one hand, and Wagner, Kant, and Schopenhauer, on the other.[24] As we have seen, Schopenhauerian pessimism had recognized itself in Empedocles. Aeschylus is evidently named because of the Wagnerian total work of art (*Gesamtkunstwerk*). As for the couple of Parmenides and Kant, more surprising at first glance, it rests upon the idea that the negation of the reality of time in Parmenides is something like an anticipation of the thesis of its ideality as this appears in Kant's Transcendental Aesthetic.

The meaning of the homology is manifest. Nietzsche wants to point out the logic of two symmetrical cultural mutations. With regard to the Greek city, the increasing decadence of the fifth century BCE, which Socrates accelerates but brings to a culmination, follows a period of flowering that Nietzsche places under the sign of tragedy. Inversely, the philosophical reform, which Schopenhauer initiated in the wake of Kant and that Wagner continued on the aesthetic level, aims to put a stop to the cultural decadence of Wilhelmine Germany by re-establishing a link with the tragic conception that Socrates had terminated within the order of philosophy just as Euripides had done within the order of drama. It is understandable that the Presocratics, to the extent that Socrates has separated himself from them, are henceforth in a position to be models for overcoming the modernity he initiated.

But this first symmetry presupposes another, more subtle one. An essential aspect of Nietzsche's analysis is that, at the very epoch of the Greek city's greatest flowering, its grandeur flourishes *in reaction* to an inherent tendency of Greek culture. This is what one might call the Hölderlinian motif in Nietzsche's analysis, even if Nietzsche could not have known the letter to Böhlendorff (1801) in which Hölderlin reformulates the aesthetic implications of the Quarrel between the Ancients and the Moderns by appealing to the notion of the "free use of what is one's own."[25] In Hölderlin, the "Hesperian" poets are able to equal the Greeks not by *developing* what is "properly their national character," but on the contrary by *resisting* it, just as the Greeks themselves had done: "for the most difficult thing," says Hölderlin, "is the *free* use of what is one's *own*."[26] For Nietzsche, in the same way, the ancient philosophers "display the vital power of this [i.e. Greek] culture, which generates its own correctives."[27] The notion of "corrective" evidently complicates the way in which the Preplatonics are invoked to serve as a paradigm, for obviously what *we* have to correct is not what *they* had to resist.

Nietzsche specifies the nature of the perils that threatened the Greeks, and to which he thinks the various philosophers responded, in one of the fragments of *The Struggle between Knowledge and Wisdom* (*Wissenschaft und Weisheit in Kampfe*, 1875):

The myth as the lazybed of thought	—against this, cold abstraction and strict science. Democritus.
The soft comfort of life	—against this, the strict ascetic conception in Pythagoras, Empedocles,
Anaximander. Cruelty in combat and struggle	—against this, Empedocles with his reform of sacrifice.
Lying and deceit	—against this, enthusiasm for the truth whatever the consequences.
Conformability, excessive sociability	—against this, Heraclitus' pride and solitude.[28]

Thus the strategy of Nietzsche's Basel lectures is double-edged. On the one hand, he defends a "scientific" vision of the world in league with the Preplatonics. At the same time, science is the response given to a specific cultural situation, something like a display of public spirit. The personal engagement of the various Preplatonics, about which Nietzsche draws upon Diogenes Laertius's *Lives and Opinions of Eminent Philosophers* to multiply the testimonia (he never forgets to emphasize that many were legislators), is itself nothing more than a sign of this "practical" dimension of the science practiced by those Greeks.

It is because of this cultural dimension that philosophy in the age of Greek tragedy is paradigmatic, even more than by reason of the particular form of its effectuation. It is true that, according to Nietzsche, the dangers weighing upon German culture are in part identical with those that Greek culture had to face, and consequently that the necessary correctives are of the same nature as those that this latter was able to apply to them during the period of its vitality: social conformability and the primacy of the collectivity are no less threatening here than they were there. But with regard to other features, what Nietzsche lists on the credit side of the Preplatonic thinkers should instead be registered on the debit side of German culture. This applies especially to the faith placed in science for combatting myth, something that Nietzsche frequently denounced. Hence, in order to understand how Nietzsche can alternately exalt the Preplatonics as a model (and he will continue to do so once he begins definitively to speak of Presocratics) and emphasize their limits, one must recognize *at the same time* the parallelisms between Greece and Germany, and the Hölderlinian structure in virtue of which what had been the Greek achievement set against an original nature has become for us the very tendency against which we must react.

In fact, if for Nietzsche the Presocratics did indeed initiate a movement of cultural reform, it remained unfinished. Socrates interrupted it *before* it arrived at its conclusion: what he shattered was in fact never more than a simple *hope*. That is why Nietzsche will be able to write in §261 of *Human All Too Human* ("The Tyrants of the Spirit"): "The sixth and fifth centuries seem always to promise more than they produced: they did not go beyond the promise and the announcement."[29] In *The Struggle between Knowledge and Wisdom*, he had put it a bit more generously: "There are still many possibilities that have not yet been discovered: that is because the Greeks did not discover them. There are other ones that the Greeks discovered and then later covered up again."[30]

Thus Nietzsche's revival of the Socratic-Ciceronian theme of Presocratic philosophy as physics and of physics as theory is traversed from the beginning by a critical movement that in fact is equivalent to its reversal. In this way, we can understand better that what the lectures pointed to as the Preplatonic philosophers' brilliant anticipations can be presented in the opening pages of *Philosophy in the Tragic Age of the Greeks* as having been just as many "errors."[31] This is not in the least incompatible with their being true, something that in any case is loudly proclaimed in the lectures. What makes their truths just so many errors is precisely the fact that these are truths that have been *surpassed*. How much does Heraclitus weigh compared with Helmholtz, or Empedocles compared with Darwin? The essence of what the Presocratics have to tell us does not have to do with their doctrine but with the relation between their doctrine and the culture within which they advanced those truths.

The germ of a more radical critique of the Presocratics was contained in embryo in the conception of the philosophers as men of science that the lectures promoted: for the value of science can be questioned—and even inverted. The pathos of truth, in which Nietzsche had at first seen an element of the Presocratics' grandeur, will soon become the name of a problem for him, as well as a privileged expression of the ascetic ideal that itself has ancient representatives too. Valorizing the *gay science* leads necessarily to diminishing the importance of a Democritus. But for the mature Nietzsche, even Empedocles no longer presents the same attraction he once had—he is still too scientific, and, which does not help matters, too democratic, without even mentioning the pessimism that aligns him with Schopenhauer. In the end, the only Presocratic who will be saved will be Heraclitus—and only barely.[32]

If Nietzsche's own problematic continued to develop, its fundamental orientation would go on to be preserved beyond him within the phenomenological tradition, especially in Heidegger. The first philosophers, representatives of the "tragic" age, had become in Nietzsche the symbol of a hoped-for postmodernity, once the victory of theoretical optimism and the primacy of morals had inaugurated this modernity (this is the reversal of the Ciceronian scheme). After Nietzsche, the Presocratics will continue to represent, of course in terms of other parameters (as it happens, reontologized ones), the visible aspect of a modernity that wonders about its crisis and its failures. In this sense, Nietzsche will turn out to have been not only "the inventor of the Presocratics," but also the greatest source of inspiration for Heidegger's "originary thinkers" (*anfängliche Denker*).[33]

Thus the Presocratics benefited from a synergy resulting from a strange alliance between historical science, represented in person by the pair Zeller/Diels, and Nietzsche's implacable critique of the historical method. In spite of this double underpinning, differently motivated scruples that are provoked by the use of the term "Presocratic" recur among the historians of Greek philosophy, and more generally among those of Archaic Greece.

If the term causes discomfort, this is due not only to the problems posed by the reference to Socrates, but also to the ambiguity and conceptual implications of the prefix. The ambiguity is twofold. First, a compound beginning with "pre-" spontaneously suggests a chronological anteriority, whereas here what is being aimed at is really, and perhaps above all (in virtue of the typological dimension of every periodization), a morphological characterization: certain Presocratics, and not the least eminent ones, are contemporaries of Socrates, and even of Plato—a contemporaneity that is all the more striking as it is during the course of a remarkable brief period, scarcely more than a century and a half, that philosophy affirms itself as a distinctive intellectual orientation. In the preface to the fifth edition of the *Fragmente der Vorsokratiker*, for which he prepared the revision, W. Kranz took care to emphasize this point: "Many contemporaries of Socrates, and certain figures who lived much later than him, appear in this work. And yet the book constitutes a unity. This latter consists in the fact that the philosophy that expresses itself here did not pass through the school of Socrates (and of Plato): thus it is not so much Presocratic philosophy as rather ancient non-Socratic philosophy."[34]

It is significant that these clarifications did not succeed in banishing all scruples. For example, it has been pointed out with regard to the Pythagorean Philolaus that "he is located on the borderline of what can be called Presocratics."[35] In fact, a morphological interpretation of the term "Presocratic" does not invalidate all chronological perspectives. An obsolete mode of thought does not generally persist for very long. Even if a periodization is not strictly supported by chronology and allows certain margins—one could even claim that these margins are essential for it[36]—nonetheless it does retain temporal implications. That is why, when the *Fragmente der Vorsokratiker* includes Pythagoreans of the Imperial period among the Presocratics, on the pretext that they are connected with the mother school, a certain misgiving is inevitable: for what distinguishes the Neo-Pythagoreans from the older ones are precisely features that are typically post-Socratic, in the present-case Academic ones.[37] If the anonymous author of the allegorical commentary discovered at Derveni in 1962, who translates an Orphic theogony into the terms of a cosmology inspired by Heraclitus, Anaxagoras, and Diogenes of Apollonia, did indeed write in the first half of the fourth century BCE (the tomb where the remains of the papyrus were found is dated within the last third of the fourth century), then he constitutes a remarkable case of belatedness, marking a limit beyond which the use of the term "Presocratic" ceases to be plausible or requires the use of quotation marks. Might belatedness, in the case of this document, be related to a certain provincialism? Derveni, in Macedonia, is not Athens, even if the discovery of such a document at Derveni can be connected with the remarkable cultural development that this region experienced during the period in question.[38]

The second source of ambiguity of the prefix "pre-" is philosophically more important. Still remaining within the temporal order, but now more ideally, the "pre-" of "Presocratic" suggests the idea of "preparation," "anticipation," indeed "inferiority." It thus constitutes a perfect expression for the teleology and the imputation of primitivism that in any case haunt the historiography of the beginnings of philosophy.

It is true that by itself the reference to Socrates as the second part of the compound term inhibited the natural tendency to make a teleological use of the prefix, since Socrates, in the Socratic-Ciceronian (and Nietzschean) tradition, stands above all for a revolution to which—whatever its parameters (practice vs. theory, human morality vs. knowledge of nature, optimism of knowledge vs. tragic

vision)—the Presocratics, so far from having prepared it, on the
contrary fall victim. And yet it is a fact that the specific reference to
Socrates is often marginalized in the use made of the term "Presocratic." In a broader sense, the anteriority of the Presocratics is understood not only in relation to Socrates, nor even in relation to
Plato (this could have been justified, given the unity of Socratic-
Platonic thought), but especially and more significantly in relation
to Aristotle: for those thinkers whom we call the Presocratics are
undeniably the main characters (though not the only ones) of the
first teleological narrative of the history of philosophy, laid down in
the first book of the *Metaphysics*: this is the deeper meaning of the
term "first philosophers."[39] This is how one can explain Nietzsche's
anti-Aristotelian attack in §261 of *Human All Too Human* ("The
Tyrants of the Spirit"): "Especially Aristotle seems not to have eyes
to see when he finds himself in the presence of these men.... It
seems that these marvellous philosophers lived in vain, or that they
had done nothing more than prepare the disputatious and garru-
lous batallions of the Socratic schools."[40] By means of this reference
to the "Socratic schools" (which are and are not Socrates "himself"),
Nietzsche succeeds in making the two determinations of "Presocratic" and "Prearistotelian" coincide, thereby revealing the underlying
logic of another, as it were non-Socratic, usage of the term "Presocratic." In fact, it all often happens as though, in the compound term,
the power of the prefix ("pre-") overcame the limitation imposed by
the root ("Socrates"). One can see why Heidegger, in some sense the
most important votary of the "Presocratics" after Nietzsche, nevertheless avoided the term and spoke of the "originary thinkers" (*die
anfänglichen Denker*).[41]

Thus it is easy to understand that the historiography of the
Presocratics after Zeller witnessed a certain number of arbitrary
attempts at reforming the terminology. Instead of "Presocratic,"
one scholar, for example, has spoken of "pre-Attic philosophy (or
period)"—an attempt at a geographical neutralization that is indirectly inspired by the distinction in Diogenes Laertius between the
two origins, Eastern ("Ionian") and Western ("Italic"), of Greek philosophy, and which rests upon the idea that it is only with Anaxag-

oras that philosophy was imported into Athens and that it was only with Archelaus, the alleged teacher of Socrates, that it managed to establish itself there.[42] One also finds "pre-Sophistic philosophy (or period)," which presupposes the Hegelian demarcation.[43] These two proposals remained without an echo—something that is worth emphasizing, given the potential attractiveness of at least the second one. "Archaic philosophy" has had more success; this is due to the degree to which the category of the "archaic," thematized at first by archaeologists and art historians in the very same years in which Nietzsche was constructing the era of tragedy as that of Greek grandeur, rapidly took charge transversely of all the phenomena, literary and philosophical, which the ideology of ideality and Classicism had obscured.[44] But none of these readjustments succeeded in imposing itself against "Presocratic." One scholar was even able to draw the conclusion that the term is so anchored in usage that it is not worth going to the trouble to look for another one.[45]

It is all the more significant that, for his part, the editor of a collection of essays on the beginnings of Greek philosophy entitled *Companion to Early Greek Philosophy* systematically removed the term "Presocratic" in favor of "first philosophers of Greece," according to the formula inspired by Aristotle.[46] By putting the accent on an essential continuity rather than on the caesura that, despite the possible teleological interpretation, constitutes the dominant tendency of the expression "Presocratics," this Aristotelian formula offered an attractive solution for uncoupling the Presocratics from the function Nietzsche had assigned them. Within this perspective, it is understandable that the phrase "the first philosophers of Greece" derives rather from the tradition of Anglo-Saxon historiography, by opposition to the "Continental" interpretation of the Presocratics.[47] Without of course excluding "turning points" and discontinuities within the history of philosophy, it puts the accent on the establishment of philosophy as such and on its essential homogeneity, beyond all its differences.

The opposition between "the Presocratics" and "the first philosophers" is not a rigid one, and the term "Presocratics" continues to be used readily without regard to the notions it tends to convey. This is due not only to the fact that these notions—which are in part irreconcilable (are the Presocratics non-Socratic because they come before Socrates, or are they the pre-Aristotelian anticipation of Aristotle?)—neutralize each other, but also to its own merits.

To begin with, "Presocratic" has the advantage of being a linguistically convenient term, whether as an epithet or as a substantive. By assigning to one and the same domain the totality of those thinkers who preceded the undeniable intellectual and spiritual watershed that was the appearance of Socrates, it marks a turning point that is evidently significant within the history of philosophical thought, an importance that expresses well, even in its exaggeration, the parallel that some authors have not hesitated to trace between Socrates and Jesus.[48] But to this intellectual reason another, material one must be added, about which there has perhaps not been sufficient reflection.

For the feeling that the "Presocratics" constitute an entity endowed with a certain homogeneity is favored by the fact that none, or almost none, of their writings is still available to us in its entirety. They are distinguished in this regard both from Socrates, who left to others the task of writing in his stead, and from Plato and Aristotle, whose works have been preserved for us, either completely (in the case of Plato) or in large part (Aristotle). Of the Presocratics we read nothing more than fragments—taking the word "fragments" here, as in *Die Fragmente der Vorsokratiker*, in a broad sense, including, besides verbal quotations, doctrinal summaries (or "doxographies"), paraphrases, commentaries, allusions, and biographical reports—in short, the totality of information, often bits and pieces, that can support an indispensable reconstruction.

The state of the corpus is explained by the history of its transmission. The Neoplatonist Simplicius still had access to a certain number of writings of the "ancients" at the end of the sixth century AD, about ten centuries after their date of composition. He tells us explicitly that he consulted the second book of the treatise of Diogenes of Apollonia, and people agree in thinking that his lengthy quotations from Parmenides, Empedocles, or Anaxagoras, especially in his commentary on the first book of Aristotle's *Physics*, derive from his reading of the original works.[49] But Simplicius himself was aware that he was safeguarding a heritage. A number of the authors whom Aristotle quoted and who for this reason interested him directly had not been recopied for a long time, whether more ancient ones like Anaximander or Anaximenes, or more recent ones like Democritus, to say nothing about other authors of lesser importance. If in the twelfth century Theodore Prodromos and John Tzetzes were still able to read Empedocles in Constantinople, they are the last absolutely certain direct eyewitnesses to the Presocratic texts. It is true that Giovanni Aurispa mentions in a letter of 1424 a manuscript of Empedocles's *Catharmoi* that he claims to have brought back to Venice together with other books from his voyage to the East, suggesting that a manuscript of Empedocles might have survived the destruction of Constantinople in 1204; but the research undertaken to rediscover it has not met with success.[50]

Thus no work of the "Presocratics" has reached us by the intermediation of the mediaeval tradition. In almost all cases, what we know about them is what other authors, who have themselves been transmitted to us, have quoted from them, or more generally said about them, in their own writings. There exist, it is true, some exceptions. The papyrological tradition (which represents, next to the medieval tradition, a second form of "direct" transmission) has sometimes enriched a corpus that we had every reason to believe was otherwise closed, and it continues to do so from time to time. The discovery at Oxyrhynchus in Egypt in 1916 of a papyrus bearing the remains of a treatise of the sophist Antiphon rightly caused a sensation. I have already mentioned the Derveni Papyrus.[51] Just as spectacular is the first publication in 1999 of papyrological fragments of Empedocles that had been waiting in the glass frames of the Egyptological Museum of Strasbourg since the beginning of the twentieth century to be read and reconstructed.[52] But these additions, instructive (and moving) as they are, change nothing in the fundamentally fragmentary character of the corpus, even if, in this case, the fragmentation results not from the practice of quotation but from the fragility of the writing support.

Other large corpora of Antiquity have disappeared, notably—to stay with philosophy—those of the Hellenistic schools: the Stoics, Skeptics, Academics, and Epicureans. Seen from a certain distance, this disappearance was not the simple effect of chance. All of these philosophies are philosophies of the losers, of those who, after having imposed themselves for some time, finally succumbed to the alliance of Platonism and Aristotelianism—this is particularly the case of Stoicism, which for a while was the philosophical *koinê* of the Empire. In a certain way, the case of the Presocratics is similar, despite—but perhaps also because of—the renewed interest that the Hellenistic schools brought to them after Socrates and Plato had surpassed them and Aristotle had absorbed them. But because of their historical situation and the symbolic meanings they conveyed —what is involved is nothing less than the "birth" of philosophy on the one hand and Socrates on the other—it is even harder to resist the feeling that it is an *epoch* of the history of the spirit that was swallowed up with the disappearance of their writings. And thus their survival in the form of fragments, contingent though that is, seems to be one of the least disputable criteria for an identity that is otherwise problematic.

CHAPTER 3

Philosophy

THE PRECEDING CHAPTER INDICATED THE VARIOUS SENSES IN
which the Presocratic philosophers could be considered Presocratic. But to what extent are they philosophers? Although Plato, especially in the *Sophist*, treated certain figures of the Archaic age as
philosophers—that is, as authors who either actually or implicitly
share definite interests or questions, ones that he recognizes as his
own (in this case, what is at stake is the question of being[1])—it is
Aristotle who officially assigns to the thinkers whom we call Presocratic the status of "first philosophers."[2] The legitimacy of this
designation can be questioned, but to do so has significant reper-
cussions for the historiography of Greek thought, at least virtually.
Because our knowledge of the Presocratic thinkers is largely shaped
directly or indirectly by Plato and especially by Aristotle, who de-
cisively orient our reading of the origins of philosophy, a strong
tendency of historical research regarding Archaic thought since the
end of the nineteenth century has been to emancipate the Presocratics from the influence of the Aristotelian filter—as Nietzsche
did, but not necessarily in the same spirit nor with the same presuppositions.[3] To this de-Aristotelization of the contents of Presocratic thought, more recent research and proposals have added a
de-Aristotelization of the philosophical form itself[4] for the sake of
alternative classificatory arrangements. Thus it has been suggested,
for example, that it would be more appropriate to call figures like
Pythagoras, Heraclitus, or Xenophanes "sages" rather than "philosophers"; that Anaximander and Anaximenes, unlike Heraclitus and
Parmenides, are scientists rather than philosophers; or that Parmenides or Empedocles can appear as what they really are, namely,

magicians and shamans, only once they have been freed from the
philosophical rationalization to which they had fallen victim.[5]

The underlying question raised by these attempts at reclassification, some of which are more justifiable than others, is in fact that
of the *differentiation* of philosophy as an autonomous discipline. I
will focus here on two aspects: more generally, the differentiation
between myth (*muthos*) and reason (*logos*); and more specifically,
the differentiation between scientific rationality and philosophical
rationality.

The emergence and development of rationality in Greece has
often been described as a departure from myth. To tell the truth,
this does not pose problems if it is understood to mean that the first
manifestations of Greek philosophy detach themselves, for example, from Hesiod's *Theogony*, which can be classified with good reason as "myth" because of the characters it puts into action and the
plot it devises, even if Hesiodic myth is of a unique genre, in some
characteristics close to philosophy, which as yet was unborn.[6] But
the formula of a passage "from myth to reason" is often taken as
implying more generally an arrival of reason that would put an end,
if not *de facto* then at least *de jure*, to all forms of mythic discourse,
henceforth considered to have been overcome. In this last interpretation, the formula is indeed problematic for reasons that are both
philosophical—involving a critique of the Enlightenment that is
shared by numerous orientations of contemporary thought—and
scholarly, involving the clarification of the interpretative categories
involved.

The re-evaluation of "myth" achieved by the German Romantics,
the critique of reason in Nietzsche and its destruction within the
framework of Heideggerian phenomenology, the denunciation of
its totalitarian character by Horkheimer and Adorno—in one way
or another all these developments put into question the idea that
reason straightforwardly followed upon myth, no matter whether
one assumed that myth is the future of reason rather than its past,
or that reason has no kind of superiority compared to myth, or
quite simply that reason does not possess any finality. For their part,
anthropology, religious studies, and comparatism have also contributed greatly to discrediting this formula, not only by providing defi-

nitions for myth that are more complex and more adequate than the ones that Enlightenment thinkers had offered, but also by lowering the claims of reason, by showing either that rationality is at work in myth itself or that there are other rationalities besides Western rationality. This explains why nowadays the formula "from myth to reason" is usually embellished with a question mark.[7] The doubts have to do with the difficulty of defining the terms "myth" and "reason" satisfactorily and thus of conceiving of some kind of "passage" from the one to the other—independently of the undeniable problems encountered by the attempt to explain in what way this passage happened historically.[8] On the other hand, there are good reasons for retaining this formula, which focuses attention on a discontinuity between old forms of thought and new ones, a discontinuity whose existence is difficult to deny and of which it is evidently important to give an account.[9]

In fact, it is perfectly possible to overcome the two difficulties mentioned. For nothing obliges us to conceive of the passage from myth to reason as a "heroic and progressive change within Greek thought,"[10] as though what was involved was the global and exhaustive subsumption of the totality of data available within a single model. The proposal would instead be to isolate a moment that, though *significant*, nonetheless, like a Weberian ideal type, knows exceptions, variations, and retreats (as Cassirer insisted in *The Myth of the State*, nothing is more dangerous than the belief that myth cannot return[11]). As for the terms "myth" and "reason" themselves, it is appropriate to use them functionally, as this frees us from the obligation of assigning them a too-narrowly determined definition. Here the concept of differentiation can offer some help.

H. Spencer was the first to use the concept of differentiation as the central element of a general theory of evolution, which he defines as a change "from an indefinite, incoherent homogeneity to a definite, coherent heterogeneity."[12] This definition is useful in that, if it is applied to the case of the differentiation between myth and reason, it suggests that there was not myth and nothing but myth *at the beginning*, and then afterwards *reason* and nothing but that, but instead that the differentiation of reason with regard to myth induces a redistribution of discursive positions by outlining a new force field and freeing new possibilities from it. Certainly, the objection could be raised that the notion of differentiation, conceived in this way, runs the risk of undermining the idea of a passage from myth to reason rather than reinforcing it. For does it not preclude the possibility of calling the initial term "myth," insofar as it supposes myth to be the product of differentiation, not an undifferentiated origin? Is not "homogeneity" precisely a condition of things that by definition is anterior to the distinction between myth and reason?

The objection is a real one, and it would be decisive if we did not take into account the *functional* character of the distinction between "myth" and "reason." How we should understand this distinction emerges from the very history of the relation between the Greek terms *muthos* and *logos*, from which the modern pair myth/reason finally arose, even if this latter does not entirely coincide with it.

For the two words are connected with the development of the semantic field of "speech."[13] *Muthos* refers originally to the "contents" of a story and tends to be opposed to *epos*, which refers instead to the "material" aspect, the "vehicle" within which speech is articulated: that is why in its earliest usages *muthos* often designates an opinion or intention, often with a performative aspect that gives it the sense of a decision, order, or suggestion.[14] But the term can also indicate the narrative that is characteristic of a "story," a usage in which it enters into competition with *logos*, a word that, still quite rare in Homer, tends for its part to occupy the place left vacant by the specialization of *epea* to mean (epic) verses, and consequently tends to designate any kind of discourse, especially discourse in prose.

A story, *muthos* or *logos*, is originally neutral with regard to the question of truth; it can be specified whether a *muthos* or a *logos* is true or false (and the specification will not seem redundant), and this will continue to be the case even later in texts that clearly postdate the specialization of *muthos* to the side of fiction and of *logos* to the side of reality. This tendency is duplicated by another parallel one, which leads *logos* to take over everything that belongs to argumentation (to reasoning by arguments) in opposition to *muthos*, which ends up taking over the heritage of narration for itself alone.[15]

Thus, within the Greek domain, the terms *muthos* and *logos* underwent a *development* and a specialization, that is, a transition from an undifferentiated condition to a differentiated one.[16] This is not a matter of obsolescence and "replacement" (though this is one of the possibilities opened up by the differentiation itself), but the formation of a semantic "field" whose pertinent elements can clearly be identified in terms of three essential oppositions: narrativity vs. argumentation; fiction vs. truth; and distant past vs. actual present. The relation myth/reason subsists, while the contents of the terms (both in their formal determinations and in their specifications) as well as the line that divides them shift.

It is in this sense that the distinction between myth and reason is not a substantial but a functional one. In such a perspective, nothing prevents myth from being capable of itself being the product of a rational activity, and inversely nothing prevents reason from being capable of becoming mythical. For such reversals we know of good examples from Antiquity. When Plato in the *Sophist* remarks that all those, pluralists or monists, who have spoken before him about being are tellers of *myth*, this is not because they did so within the framework of a theological narration (even if this is indeed the case for some of them), but because they all answer the question of the number of beings without having asked themselves what the term "is" means: their mythology consists in not raising the appropriate questions.[17] In the first book of the *Metaphysics*, Aristotle distinguishes the first philosophers from the theologians, who also have recourse to myths, on the basis of a *different* criterion, an intrinsic one: the former had as their object "nature," whereas the latter did not.[18] But Epicurus, in a way that, to the modern reader, can suggest the dialectic of Enlightenment thinkers, reverses this determination by applying the term "myth" to a certain type of dogmatic naturalism that, in order to give an account of the phenomena, arbitrarily selects one explanation when several ones agree with the sense data.[19] Here myth is simply the price that has to be paid when the principles of a definite epistemology are not respected.

The fact that the relation between myth and reason is functional and hence flexible evidently does not mean that reason cannot be globally characterized by a certain number of ideal-typical features by which it is opposed to myth—on the contrary. With regard to philosophical rationality, one might suggest that its first expressions aim to embrace a definite content (a certain totality, of which the natural universe is the most manifest specification, even if it is not the only possible one) by means of a type of specific arguments that, negatively, does not involve the traditional divinities (while all the same being capable of reassigning to them a determinate role within a reconstructed world) and which, positively, involves a new type of reason, for which the most visible grammatical index is the increasing use of the explanatory connective particle "for" (*gar*), even if it is true that many Presocratic arguments remain implicit. Within this pair, the two terms are not symmetrical, given that the history of the development of philosophy is always also a history of the relation between the content and the form of thought and, at the end, of the transition from first-order thinking to second-order thinking— the transition for which Plato's *Phaedo* gives the credit to Socrates.[20] If we bear in mind the specifications indicated above, there is no reason not to describe this movement as a transition from *muthos* to *logos*.

As for the differentiation between science and philosophy, this has been the object of two contrasting analyses. For some scholars have maintained that the specialization of science and philosophy happened very early, starting at the end of the sixth and the beginning of the fifth century, when one can already find, next to "pure" philosophers like Heraclitus, "pure" scientists like the astronomer Cleostratus of Tenedos or the historian and geographer Hecataeus of Miletus—and if we follow Mansfeld's suggestion, mentioned above,[21] the term would also be applicable to Anaximander and Anaximenes, who in that case would have to be considered cosmologists and not philosophers. The fifth century would merely have deepened this specialization, especially in the domain of science, with first-rate mathematicians like Hippocrates of Chios, Theodorus of Cyrene, and Theaetetus, none of whom left any trace of philosophical studies; astronomers like Oenopides of Chios, Meton, and Euctemon of

Athens; and doctors, many of whose treatises are devoted to purely scientific questions.[22]

But it has also been maintained that the disciplinary classifications and distinctions to which, often following the ancients, we spontaneously recur—such as philosophy, wisdom, sophistic, history, nature, medicine, mathematics—are misleading, insofar as the activities subsumed under these terms do not belong to an intellectual and scientific field that was already differentiated.[23] To take the most favorable case, that of mathematics, it is true that a figure like Hippocrates of Chios suggests a certain specialization, insofar as he devotes himself entirely to the resolution of mathematical problems. But can one infer from this the existence of a category of ancient "mathematicians," of which Hippocrates, Euctemon, and Meton would be the representatives? Two sets of reasons suggest that this might be doubted. The first, negative one is that in fact we know practically nothing about Euctemon, and that Meton, to follow Aristophanes's portrait of him, makes one think of an encyclopedic spirit in the tradition of Thales rather than of a specialist.[24] The second, more important one is that there are nonmathematicians who work "professionally" in the domain of mathematics, like Antiphon, Bryson, or Democritus.[25] As for medicine, in fact the Hippocratic corpus reflects very varied interests that cannot easily be reduced to a specialized conception of medicine, since cosmological, linguistic, or ethnological questions are discussed in it and not only more narrowly medical ones.[26]

These factors led G. E. R. Lloyd to speak of the "complexity of the map of intellectual activities in the 6th and 5th centuries" and of the "difficulty of assigning particular individuals to neatly defined categories, whether we use their categories or our own." He went on: "that is true for 'philosophers' no less than for 'mathematicians' and 'doctors.' Disciplinary boundaries before Plato remained both disputed and flexible."[27]

There is only a single step from here to denying that there is something like a Preplatonic philosophy, and some scholars have not hesitated to take that step. Thus it has been maintained that "the discipline of philosophy ... was not born, like a natural organism.

Rather, it was an artificial construct that had to be invented and le-
gitimized as a new and unique cultural practice. This took place in
Athens in the fourth century BCE, when Plato appropriated the
term 'philosophy' for a new and specialized discipline—a discipline
that was constructed in opposition to the many varieties of *sophia* or
'wisdom' recognized by Plato's predecessors and contemporaries."[28]

Now, while no one would even think of denying that Plato or
Socrates impressed their mark deeply upon the definition and practice of philosophy (in this derivative sense, one can even say that
they were its inventors), using the vocabulary of artificiality in opposition to a model of natural and organic growth misses what is
essential to a cultural process like the emergence of philosophy—
even aside from the fact that the thesis of a Platonic invention of the
discipline of philosophy rests upon a controversial factual basis, as
we shall see in a moment. Even admitting that no branch of knowledge is already truly specialized in the Presocratic period, one can
hardly deny that a certain *process* of specialization can be recognized. And precisely that is the interesting phenomenon.

The nature of this process cannot be understood by opposing
fluidity or complexity to the static category of specialization, for
these are no less static. The dynamic of specialization manifests
itself as a necessarily heterogeneous process, each discipline pos-
sessing its own prehistory, its own conditions and rhythms of development, and its own way of interacting with the other branches of
knowledge. Philosophy, moreover, is doubtless more exposed to
constant reconfigurations than other disciplines are, because of the
very fact of the relative indeterminacy of its "object." There are doctors in Homer, as elsewhere; there had been Babylonian astronomers and mathematicians. In spite of the radical differences between Homeric doctors and Hippocratic ones, between Babylonian
astronomy and Greek astronomy, it seems difficult to deny that at
a certain level they both concern an identifiable object (wounds and
disease, astronomical phenomena). Matters are different in the case
of philosophy, for here an object or, perhaps better, a set of totally
new problems had to be conceived, and not only a new approach
concerning a content that was already relatively well circumscribed.
The relation between *sophos* and *philosophos* is doubtless not the

same as the one between protoastronomers and astronomers, and this is why the question of the origin of philosophy and the transition from wisdom to philosophy poses itself so insistently, both for the ancients and for us.[29]

Incomplete as our information about the terms "philosopher," "philosophize," and "philosophy" is, we know enough about them to say that they begin to be used in a quasi-technical sense in the last third of the fifth century, at the very moment when the "inquiry into nature" begins to be designated as such.[30] But this does not mean that one cannot or should not go back further in the one case as in the other. Contrary to a widespread presupposition, the criterion of the existence of an activity or representation is not furnished by the existence of the corresponding word. For language can be inventive, but it also possesses its own inertia. If neologisms are always possible, occasionally some time must also pass before language reflects a certain change in practice, in virtue of a principle of linguistic belatedness. It is important that we be able to continue to describe as "philosophical" a certain intellectual approach that preceded the appearance of the concept, indeed that of the word itself.

As for the ancients, they tended to see the thing as emerging together with the word.[31] So one can easily understand that the invention of the term "philosophy" could have been attributed to Pythagoras in relation with a conception of philosophy understood as a theoretical activity (this is the explanation he gives to the tyrant Leon, already mentioned in the first chapter[32]). It has been suggested that this word, which is found (though this is controversial) in a fragment of Heraclitus (hence at the turn of the sixth and fifth centuries) does indeed go back to Pythagoras, and this would bring us to the end of the sixth century. But it seems more reasonable to think, with the majority of scholars, that what we have here is a retrospective projection, doubtless derived in the present instance from Pythagorean influence on the Platonic Academy.[33]

In any case, the word *philosophos*, which neither Homer nor Hesiod could use for metrical reasons anyway, is a relatively recent creation, and the first uses made of it that we can be certain of, toward the middle of the fifth century, are far from suggesting the idea of any kind of philosophical discipline: this is so much the case that the "philosophers," when they appropriate the word, will have to distinguish themselves sharply from what the term designated. The most famous case, which others may have preceded (Heraclitus, according to a possible interpretation of Frag. B35 DK = D40 LM[34]), is that of Plato, who in book 5 of the *Republic* opposes the true *philosophoi*, etymologically analyzed within a Socratic-Platonic perspective as "those who love wisdom," to merely curious people who usurp the term and whom, Plato suggests, it would be better to call *philotheamones* ("those who love to watch").[35]

For, to begin with, "to philosophize" means according to the context "to display curiosity," "to cultivate one's mind," "to love discussion."[36] When Thucydides has Pericles attribute one of the causes of the supremacy of the Athenians to the fact that "we practice philosophy without falling into softness," what he is pointing to is a culture of debate and of aesthetic judgment.[37] A generation earlier, it is the intellectual open-mindedness and experience of the world that made Croesus, king of Lydia, say that Solon of Athens, who was visiting his court, "practiced philosophy":

> "When he [i.e. Solon] had observed everything and examined it, Croesus took the opportunity and said, 'Athenian stranger, you have a great reputation among us on account of your wisdom and your wanderings, since, practicing philosophy [i.e. in your desire for knowledge], you have traveled much of the earth for the sake of observation.'"[38]

The idea that "philosophers" are great lovers of knowledge, curious about the things of the world, and consequently inclined to travel, is probably likewise present in the fragment of Heraclitus referred to above,[39] which, if the text printed by the majority of editors is accepted, connects "philosophy" to curiosity: "men who love wisdom [*philosophoi*] must be investigators into very many things."[40] Two readings are available, and one must choose between them. Either Heraclitus is attacking what he violently rejects elsewhere as "much learning [*polymathiê*]."[41] In this case, "to philosophize" as Solon does is precisely what one must avoid doing. Or, with a gesture that would anticipate the Platonic criticism of book 5 of the *Republic*, he is affirming that, in order to philosophize truly, one must doubtless have seen many things—but that this is not enough. In the one case, this fragment of Heraclitus will reflect a decisive moment in the appropriation of an available term by an activity that was currently in the process of differentiating itself; in the other, it will only provide evidence of the process by which "philosophy," in the technical meaning of the term, constructed itself in a way that was still anonymous against what it had been hitherto (a curiosity for the world, destined to become simple curiosity).[42] Both interpretations evidently presuppose that Heraclitus really did use the term "philosopher." It is indicative of the problems raised by the apparent use of the term at such an early date that some scholars have suggested that it might be nothing more than a gloss by Clement of Alexandria, the author who cites the passage, and that it would be better to expel it from the original text.[43]

In fact, the data, relatively few in number but significant, point once again toward the last third of the fifth century as the period when the words "philosopher" and "philosophy" came to refer to an activity of a specific type—which does not mean that they were indicating a kind of "specialized" study. As far as can be judged from Plato's dialogues and Xenophon, Socrates already made a distinctive use of the term in this period, linking philosophy to the search for happiness in a protreptic perspective. But setting Socrates aside, there are at least three witnesses to an undeniable specialization of the term toward this same date.

The first passage, in chapter 20 of the Hippocratic treatise *On Ancient Medicine*, was already quoted in the first chapter with regard to the "inquiry into nature."[44] It is particularly interesting in the present context because it contains the first attestation of the abstract substantive *philosophia*:

> Certain doctors and sophists [or: experts] say that it is impossible for anyone to know medicine who does not know what a human being is…. But what they are talking about belongs to philosophy, like Empedocles or others who have written about nature: what a human being is from the beginning, how he first appeared and out of what things he is constituted. But as for me, I think that whatever has been said or written by some expert or

doctor about nature belongs less to the art of medicine than to
that of painting [*graphikê*], and I think that there is no other
source than medicine for having some clear knowledge about
nature.

One of the problems this passage poses is whether *graphikê*—
the art with which this traditionalist medical writer compares philosophy, to the latter's disadvantage—is to be understood as "painting" or instead as "writing" (indeed as "literature"). For the verb
graphein can mean "to paint" as well as "to write." In favor of the
translation given here, one can assign importance to the fact that
the substantive *graphikê*, which in the fourth century is only attested
in the sense of painting, already possessed this established meaning
at the end of the fifth century.[45] Moreover, a rapprochement between philosophy and painting, surprising as it might seem at first,
appears to be more appropriate in this context than one between
philosophy and writing. It is not, as has been proposed, that the
rapprochement was suggested by the mention of Empedocles, who
in his poem on nature had compared Aphrodite—one of the names
of the power that he more often calls Love, who engenders the infinite variety of natural forms by starting from the four elementary
"roots"—to artists, who obtain the variety of pictorial forms by starting from basic colors.[46] Such an allusion would only be meaningful
if Empedocles's Aphrodite practiced philosophy herself (but this is
not the case), to say nothing of the fact that this medical writer is
aiming less at Empedocles than at the genetic approach that he represents, which consists in going back to the origins, and which the
analogy of the painter's palette does not illustrate. It seems rather
that within the framework of this treatise, which is directed against
a speculative type of medicine that is accused of operating on the
basis of illegitimate presuppositions,[47] painting is being considered
as the very example of an art of *representation*, and thus as being
purely "theoretical" in comparison with the art of medicine, whose
goal is to cure or alleviate.[48] This criticism, which is aimed at philosophy's approach as such, would be even more scathing with regard
to Empedocles, who had emphatically made a point of the effective-

ness of his knowledge, illustrated by its thaumaturgic power to "bring out of Hades the strength of a man who has died."[49]

However this point is to be understood, the passage of *Ancient Medicine* not only illustrates a double "disciplinary" conflict, internal and external (within medicine itself, and between medicine and philosophy), but also attests a use of "philosophy" by virtue of which the term refers to those who study "nature," even if in an illegitimate manner.

The second text that is relevant in this context is §13 of Gorgias's *Encomium of Helen*, which, discussing the power of persuasion, distinguishes three domains of discursive activity: the arguments (*logoi*) of "those who study the heavens [*meteôrologoi*]"; the contentions (*agônes*) of the parties involved in a trial; and finally philosophical contests (*hamillai*). Given that meteorology here in all likelihood represents by a frequent synecdoche the inquiry into nature in general,[50] the people whom Gorgias calls "meteorologists" in this passage largely overlap—indeed, coincide—with the naturalists whom the author of *Ancient Medicine* accuses of devoting themselves to philosophy. Gorgias himself uses the term "philosophize" for something else, namely, for a specific form of argumentative competition. Manifestly, what Gorgias has in mind here is dialectical controversy as we know it from the Platonic dialogues and Aristotle's *Topics*, in which what is involved is not a particular domain of reality (like the world) but *any* subject that can give rise to a debate.[51]

To these two direct testimonia must be added another one supplied by Plato's *Euthydemus* concerning the definition of the term *sophistês* given by the "sophist" Prodicus, who was known for having systematically distinguished the senses of synonyms. Before the contraction this word underwent because of Plato's polarization between sophistry and philosophy, it had designated quite generally the "expert"—a more technical and more modern figure than the ancient "sages":[52] this is its meaning in the passage of *Ancient Medicine* quoted above (where it is translated as "sophists [or: experts]"), or in Diogenes of Apollonia, who still called *sophistai* those people who in his time ought already to have been known under the name of "naturalists."[53] Now Prodicus, to follow the report of the *Euthydemus*, said about the sophist that he occupied the "boundary between the philosopher and the statesman."[54] This definition, in locating sophistic pratice at the point of articulation between the two great orientations of human activity—study (eminently represented by philosophy) and action (eminently represented by politics)—also presupposes a vision of philosophy as an essentially theoretical activity, just as in *Ancient Medicine*. This is not only interesting because Prodicus, whom we classify as a sophist, was describing the sophist in an unheard-of way that evidently anticipates Plato's own, but also because the metaphor of the boundary (*methoria*) provides evidence of an awareness, which we may call indigenous, of a process of specialization that was going on, and of the typological debate bearing upon it.

One can conclude on the basis of these passages that toward the last third of the fifth century, philosophy had become an activity identifiable as such. This does not mean that the object of philosophical activity had been precisely circumscribed. On the contrary, philosophy refers in one case to the study of nature (*Ancient Medicine*), in another to dialectical contest (Gorgias), in the third to theoretical activity (Prodicus), and it is known that Socrates himself saw in it the only means capable of providing human happiness. What is to be done with this diversity of characterizations? One consideration, which should surely not be underestimated despite its apparent triviality, is that by its nature philosophy is a discipline whose boundaries are more open than those of other disciplines are, so that there is a specific difficulty in defining its proper object. Powerful evidence for the fact that, however variously diversity can be conceived, this does not in the least prejudice the homogeneity of "philosophical" activity, is the fact that this remains no less valid after philosophy has acquired a disciplinary status than it was before. The heterogeneity among the various Presocratics is not different from the one that separates Socrates from Plato, Plato from Aristotle, Hegel from Kierkegaard, Frege from Heidegger. If there exists something like styles and forms of thought, it follows that morphological diversity, like professional diversity, is too weak a criterion to distinguish between what is "philosophy" and what is not.[55] This remains true *even* for the beginnings—which does not mean that, to an extent that it is difficult to define, the relative lack of differentiation between intellectual activities could not *also* have contributed to the heterogeneity of philosophical productions.

In any case, it is important to distinguish between external differentiation and internal differentiation. The fact that one social group differentiates itself from another one does not at all imply that it is homogeneous itself, indeed quite the contrary (the same applies to an organ). Self-assertion in the face of the environment is regularly, indeed necessarily, accompanied by internal divisions and confrontations ("potter is angry with potter," said Hesiod[56]) and hence also by internal distinctions—which means paradoxically that the trespassing of existing boundaries belongs to the process of their definition. This is doubtless eminently true of philosophy, by reason of its particular inherent plasticity.

One reason for this plasticity has to do with the distinctive interest of philosophy in totalities and generalities whose contours can be redefined at every moment (this could even be considered a major principle of the dynamic of philosophical thought). Evidence for this is provided by philosophy's vocation to embrace the specialized disciplines at a certain level. Chapter *Lambda* 8 of the *Metaphysics*, which is all the more interesting as Aristotle recognizes explicitly here the possibility that the philosopher might not have the last word in questions of astronomy (though he does not exclude this either), provides a good illustration of the tensions resulting from this configuration.[57] But Aristotle is working within an environment in which the disciplines have already been largely differentiated. The data concerning the Presocratics are much more difficult to evaluate, since one hardly ever encounters an explicit discussion or statement of a position concerning the relation between philosophy and other disciplines.

An interesting case is the detailed description that Diogenes of Apollonia provides for the system of veins (and arteries) in the human body in a long fragment that Aristotle quotes in his *History of Animals*.[58] From the indications of Simplicius, who, without quoting the passage, manifestly alludes to it when he invokes "his detailed anatomical description of the vessels,"[59] it emerges clearly that this text comes from the first book of Diogenes's treatise. It is

significant that certain scholars have nonetheless attributed the passage either to the second book of the same treatise, in which physiology was discussed, or else to another work of Diogenes, entitled
"On the Nature of Man" (*Peri phuseôs anthrôpou*).[60] The discussion
betrays a certain hesitation regarding the fragment's status: "philosophical" or "physiological"? The fact that it is transmitted by Aristotle in a work on zoology, in a chapter dedicated to blood and to
the blood vessels, is also eloquent, because one might wonder to
what extent Aristotle's treatise itself, which is the context of the
quotation, is or is not of a philosophical nature (to the degree that
this question makes sense). Aristotle quotes Diogenes's description
between a short one from a certain Syennesis, whom Aristotle identifies as "the doctor of Cyprus," and one from Polybus, a well-known
disciple of Hippocrates. Manifestly, Aristotle quotes Diogenes on
the same level as he does professional doctors. It is not certain that
he was in fact a doctor. But even if this was the case, it is quite clear
that there is a "philosophical" reason for the care that Diogenes
takes in describing the vessels that permeate the bodies of living
beings. For Diogenes's fundamental thesis is that the principle, that
is, air, is "intelligent," and the way in which its intelligence is en-
hanced or hindered constitutes an important part of the demonstration he elaborated in favor of this thesis. This is the reason why
he assigns such great importance to the existence of a network
thanks to which air and blood are distributed "throughout the whole
body"[61] (since Diogenes's vessels transport not only blood but also
air, and in fact even more of the latter than of the former): sensation
and thought ("intelligence," in the global sense in which Diogenes
uses the term) depend upon this distribution, which also explains
certain physiological functions like digestion, reproduction, and
sleep.[62] It could be said that in the case of Diogenes, doing philosophy implies doing medicine in the same sense in which, in the case
of Aristotle, doing philosophy implies doing astronomy, at least up
to a certain point.

A history of the way in which philosophy differentiated itself must
operate with a certain idea of what is supposed to differentiate itself, and thus presupposes some criterion of demarcation between

science and philosophy. Such a criterion can be more or less strong. An extreme position consists in distinguishing scientific problems from philosophical problems, where the former are in principle capable of receiving a solution, but the latter are not.[63] Among the weaker criteria that have been, or could be, proposed figure the recourse to demonstration or experimentation, the use of empirical data, that of rational argumentation, or again simply the secular character of the procedure adopted. Evidently these criteria cannot pretend to an absolute value, and it is easy to play the ones off against the others. Against Popper's elevation of the Presocratics into a paradigm of scientific debate, conceived as a space of critical discussion proceeding by the falsification of a theory,[64] his opponents have pointed out that empiricism played only a small role among the Presocratic philosophers, while other scholars have recalled that, if what is at stake is Greek science, medicine has more to teach us than the naturalists' speculations.[65] In fact, the distinction between science and philosophy calls for a discussion analogous to that regarding the distinction between myth and reason: a functional approach is just as advisable here as there. For it is vain to wish to assign the inquiry into nature exclusively to science (a certain type of science) or to philosophy: since it was eventually to give birth to both, it is neither the one nor the other, and it can fall under the one description or the other according to the angle from which it is considered.

It has sometimes been asked whether it would not be better, despite Aristotle, to make philosophy begin with Parmenides rather than with Thales, who instead would represent the beginning of *scientific* thought, like his two Milesian successors (Anaximander and Anaximenes).[66] The argument is that we do not have the same conception of the relation between philosophy and science as Aristotle did. Aristotle opens a tradition of which Descartes, Pascal, and Leibniz are still representative, for which natural science is an integral part of philosophy (this remains true at least until the eighteenth century). Thus he has no difficulty in considering the Presocratics as philosophers insofar as they are men of science. This would no longer be the case for us, as we make a much sharper distinction between the two domains.

This proposal illustrates perfectly the point, which, though trivial, is no less true, that we cannot identify an activity as philosophical unless it corresponds to what at a given moment is recognized as philosophical. But it must be pointed out that it does not square with the argument that Aristotle explicitly elaborates. For if Aristotle presents Thales as the founder of a new way of philosophizing, this is not because he cultivates one branch of philosophy that can be identified as natural philosophy or science. Almost to the contrary, it would be more correct to say that if Thales is a representative of natural *philosophy* for Aristotle, it is because he elaborates for the first time a theory of the substrate (indeed of substance), to which Aristotle gives the name "nature."[67]

So are there features common to philosophical activity, ones less specific than the one Aristotle indicates in the passage of the *Metaphysics* mentioned just now, that can explain how it came to be perceived as an independent discipline? Besides the fact that, from the point of view of a certain shared meaning or practice, *philosophia*, which was connected from the beginning to visual curiosity, lent itself easily to designating any kind of theoretical inquiry, and in a purely descriptive sense (as is suggested perhaps by the comparison between philosophy and painting in the treatise on *Ancient Medicine*), there are two parameters that, taken together, allow us to recognize the complex synergy that was necessary for the differentiation of a new type of intellectual activity, and in this sense for a genuine specialization, even before the term "philosophy" came to ratify the birth of a new discipline. The two parameters are these: first, totalization, which, following the ancient descriptions, can be considered as a characteristic of the inquiry into nature,[68] even if it is not distinctive of it (the ambition of Hesiod's *Theogony* is no less totalizing); and second, a certain type of rationalization, in which the substantial aspect of the deployment of natural entities to the detriment of the gods of myth, which certainly plays a driving role if not an exclusive one, encounters another aspect, one that is more general and more formal, namely argumentation.

CHAPTER 4

Rationality

SOME GREEKS WERE AWARE THAT THEY HAD INHERITED MUCH of their knowledge, and indeed even many of their modes of thought, from other peoples who did not speak Greek and who, for this reason, the Greeks called "barbarians."[1] The thesis of the barbarian origin of philosophy goes back to the Platonic Academy and Aristotle and has antecedents in the catalogue of parallels that the sophist Hippias of Elis established between statements made by Greek authors and those of barbarians.[2] It is this thesis that Diogenes Laertius seems to attack with evident acrimony in the prologue of his *Lives and Opinions of Eminent Philosophers*.[3] But from a historical point of view, there can be no doubt that there was an Oriental influence, which is easily explained by the geographical and historical configuration (and not only if the beginnings of Greek philosophy are located in Miletus[4]), even if this was obscured for a long time, partly for lack of documentation (it was only gradually that discoveries intervened), partly for ideological reasons having to do with the status of Greece in the self-representation of Western culture. Nowadays we are in a better position to appreciate this influence.[5] The Milesian cosmologies, which are of a kind unheard of earlier in the Greek world, are undeniably marked in some of their features by Oriental models (Mesopotamian, Iranian). Among the more general patterns, one can cite, for example, the great originary separations that make distinct entities emerge from primeval indistinction,[6] and, at a more concrete level, certain cosmogonic or cosmographic representations. Thales's originary water, on which the earth floats like a boat, has its counterpart in an Akkadian cosmology and in *Genesis*.[7] The three circles (or "skies") that divide Anaximander's universe recall an Akkadian text that can be dated to the middle of the seventh century, in which the stars occupy the lower sky, while the striking distribution of the heavenly bodies in Anaximander's cosmos (with the stars closest to us, then the moon, and the sun farthest away of all) recalls an Iranian text.[8] Anaximenes's comparison of the stars to "images" (*zôgraphêmata*) fastened onto a crystalline vault strongly recalls a passage of the *Enuma Elis* in which Marduk draws on a sky of jasper "the constellations of the gods," as well as an astronomical text entitled *Enuma Anu Enlil*.[9] Rapprochements like this can be, if not multiplied (for the documentation remains limited), at least increased. It has even been suggested that forms of rationalization, indeed of naturalization, that scholars often consider as a distinctive mark of the first Greek cosmologists, can be found in a series of Mesopotamian texts of an "explanatory" type.[10] In any case it remains true that the first Greek cosmologies stand at the origin of intellectual developments that, all scholars agree, no longer have a counterpart in the Near East. The fact that the "Greek miracle" must be put back into the context of what Burkert has called the "Orientalizing period" of Greek culture does not exclude recognition of their radical novelty, which the anachronistic application of the term "philosophy" to them suggests in its own way.[11] Burkert, who has militated so strongly for contextualizing the origins of Greek thought, provides a fine example of the way in which the new emerges from the old, upon which it continues to depend, when he remarks that when Anaximander combines the three Akkadian skies with the three categories of heavenly bodies (stars, moon, sun), he in fact introduces the entirely novel question "about sizes and distances in astronomy," which can legitimately be called "rational."[12] There is a *use* of inherited representations here, and an irreducible novelty. As Burkert himself says at the conclusion of his analysis, "In the end, the Greek achievement is certainly unique, even if we are reluctant to speak of a Greek miracle."[13] It is important to point out that the Greek contribution can be recognized not only at the level of contents but also, and probably even more, at the level of the modes of their production: the fact that the new Milesian cosmologies follow one after another in relatively brief intervals during the course of the sixth century provides evidence for a systematic practice of self-positioning with regard to views or theses that had been formulated earlier, and for a remarkable acceleration of reflection, which is undeniably a fundamental aspect of the development of a new rationality.[14]

If rationality then was not born in Greece, the problem of the origins of Greek philosophy cannot be separated from the question of the emergence of *Greek* rationality. To this last question J.-P. Vernant gave a memorable and influential answer in *The Origins of Greek Thought* more than sixty years ago by connecting the development of this rationality to the formation of the city (*polis*).[15] One might wonder to what extent this answer, whose meaning and implications are far from being evident, can contribute to understanding the kind of rationality that is specific to philosophy. It is all the more necessary to raise this question since Vernant's analysis of the emergence of rationality depends strongly upon the particular case of philosophy.

Vernant's program is largely motivated by his concern to put an end to the idea of a "Greek miracle." The phrase was coined by Ernest Renan,[16] but Vernant's use of it cannot be reduced to its inventor's. In Renan, the Greek miracle is a category that is at the same time both aesthetic and axiological: it signifies the perpetuity of the beautiful within the tradition of Classical humanism and universalism. It was with regard to the temples of Selinunte that Renan wrote in 1875, "Every attempt, every groping is visible, and, more extraordinary than the rest: when the creators of this marvelous art had achieved perfection, they no longer changed anything in it. This is the miracle that only the Greeks knew how to accomplish: to discover the ideal, and, once they had discovered it, to hold on to it."[17] Even more clearly, the page that introduces Renan's celebrated "Prayer which I said on the Acropolis when I had succeeded in understanding the perfect beauty of it" evokes the "Greek miracle," next to the "Jewish miracle," as "a thing which has only existed once, which had never been seen before, which will never be seen again, but the effect of which will last for ever, an eternal type of beauty, without a single blemish, local or national."[18] Such a miracle is not at all incompatible with a process of maturation and development, which Renan even mentions explicitly in the first of the two passages just cited. The miracles that Vernant attacks for his part presuppose on the contrary that Greek reason arose suddenly, ignorant of any "attempt" and "groping," without any preparation or origin, "just as the scales falls from the eyes of a blind mind."[19] One could also say, since what is involved is the establishment of a genealogy: like the Immaculate Conception.

The problem Vernant inherited from I. Meyerson, the founder of the "historical psychology"[20] to which he always professed allegiance, is of an epistemological order: to give an account, within the perspective of a history conceived as being essentially "fragmented," of discontinuity in history—a discontinuity of which there are many other examples, but of which the political and intellectual upheavals of Greece in the sixth and fifth centuries, with the appearance of new forms of political organization, new mathematics, new types of thought like philosophy, and of course artistic wonders, offer the historian a paradigm no less pregnant that does, for example, the French Revolution. Later the historian C. Meier coined the phrase with regard to the invention of democracy: "The Greeks had no Greeks to emulate. They were therefore unaware of the possibility of democratic government before they created it themselves."[21] This insistence on discontinuity explains why Vernant's criticisms are directed not only against the Christian version of the Greek miracle, which has at least the merit of recognizing the existence of a rupture, but also against the position of the Cambridge anthropologists known as the "ritualists," and in particular against Cornford, who himself subverted the Victorian idealizations of Greece by one-sidedly stressing the *continuities* existing between mythic thought and rational thought, and hence the dependence of the latter upon the former.[22] Against the double illusion of birth *ex nihilo* and of the resilience of the identical, Vernant has recourse to the category of "revolution," or, following Meyerson's terminology, of "mutation."[23] The terms indicate change, a considerable one (against the ritualists); but what is involved is not a miracle, because a mutation, like consciousness, is always a mutation *of something*.

Thus rational thought has a genealogy, or, as Vernant says in 1957, in an article entitled "The Formation of Positive Thought in Archaic Greece," a civil status, something that presupposes a place and date of *birth*: to state that rational thought is the "daughter of the city" is to put an end to the "Greek miracle."[24]

Vernant's analysis is based on the representative but partial case of the origins of science and philosophy. In this, he follows Louis Gernet, his second mentor next to Meyerson, who, himself already open to the Meyersonian problematic, had in his last writings drawn attention to the interest of the philosophical corpus within the framework of studies bearing on the origins of the Greek city.[25]

Vernant summarizes the novelty of the Presocratic cosmologies in two terms, *positivity* and *publicity*, of which the former points to the contents of these new productions, the latter to their form. Following up on the argument of an article by Gernet entitled "The Origins of Greek Philosophy," Vernant's demonstration is based essentially on the Ionian thinkers for the former aspect and on the philosophers of Magna Graecia for the latter one. This division, which deploys in its own way the bipartition by which Diogenes Laertius structures his *Lives and Opinions of Eminent Philosophers*, is not free of a certain artificiality, since Vernant does not ask why the East is more interesting for the contents and the West for the form (if indeed this was the case).[26] But if we examine each of these two determinations for themselves and as being virtually applicable to all the protophilosophers, independently of their geographical origin, we are led to pose the problem of their relation in other, perhaps more pertinent, terms.

"Positivity"—the concept is inherited from Auguste Comte—designates a process of "naturalization" that, Vernant maintains, occurs at one and the same time with regard to both the divine and the social worlds: it is not only that the Presocratic natural philosophers, in their tendency toward abstraction, do not have recourse to the traditional gods (in fact, in certain cases these can become the objects of allegorical explanations); but, what is more, the narrative of the origins is no longer, as it once could be, a moment of justification of the social order—a social order defined much earlier, during the Mycenean era, by the figure of a priest-king ruling over an undivided world.[27] What the positive narrative attests to, according to Vernant, is thus not only a process of secularization, but also—to use a vocabulary that is not his own—one of autonomization and differentiation of the two spheres of nature and politics.[28] As for the formal conditions for the exercise of philosophy, these have to do with the fact that philosophical debate (like other kinds of debate) is inscribed within the public space—an inscription that is all the more evident as the contents themselves often bear the traces of shamanic or mystic antecedents, particularly in Magna Graecia.[29]

Vernant assigns particular importance to the fact that in its two dimensions, positivity and publicity, Greek philosophy has counterparts in all the sectors of social organization, according to a parallelism that Gernet already emphasized. Whether it is a matter of politics, economics, or laws, the same process of abstraction and democratization is at work, in Cleisthenes's reform, the birth of coinage, and new legal institutions.[30] Considering the various sectors that are constitutive of human activity, one is struck by the pervasive consistency ("*solidarité*") of the changes, which can be considered as being just as many manifestations of one and the same rationality.

"Pervasive consistency" is the keyword here, the one that justifies going back and forth between the general category of "rational thought" and its various specifications (including philosophy). This is not the Marxist theory of reflection. Although Vernant's analysis bears unmistakable Marxist features, he refuses the simplification that would, for example, turn the identity of being into a direct transposition of the notion of monetary value.[31] On the contrary: basing himself once again upon Meyerson (whose attention was directed just as much to specificities as to discontinuities), he insists upon the *specificity of the elaborations* in each of the fields considered.[32] Nonetheless, it remains true that all these elaborations can be referred to a common basis that could be qualified as "focal" in the language of Aristotle's interpreters:[33] just as all of the meanings of being as they are declined in the categories are related to the focus represented by the first of them, substance, so too all the manifestations of the new Greek rationality find their meaning and ultimate ground in the city, this entirely novel form of organization.

The question has been raised whether the miracle that had been expelled through the door might not re-enter by the window, by being simply displaced from the origins of rational thought to the origins of the city.[34] Vernant is surely not liable to this objection, since the city is itself merely the result of a long process whose stages can be traced, at least in their larger features, which means going back all the way to the collapse of Mycenean society. This is also why his book entitled *The Origins of Greek Thought* is not a book about the Presocratic philosophers or their immediate predecessors, as the title might suggest, but about the socio-psychological conditions that presided over the emergence of the city. By contrast, it is certain that going back to the origins of the city in this way does not coexist comfortably with the thesis of the emergence of Greek rationality as a daughter *of the city*. C. Meier put his finger on one of the major difficulties of Vernant's position when he pointed out that the "birth of the political" in circumstances that are marked, in archaic Greece, by an "extreme contingency" cannot be explained without appealing to the driving role of *reflection* (especially of "political" reflection)—that is to say, of a kind of thought that still owes nothing to politics, which on the contrary it had to make possible in the first place.[35] More generally, the relation between the city and its daughter is not more transparent than the one between the spirit of Protestantism and capitalism, as Max Weber envisaged it: Is this a question of causality, of conditions of possibility, of a propitious factor, of elective affinities, or of simple analogy?

Doubtless it is futile to seek an answer to this question in Vernant, who does not seem ever to have truly paid attention to the resources and questions that Weber's problematic makes available, despite the fact that Weber too asserts a thesis about the origin of rationality—even if in his case what is involved is the emergence of modern rationality.[36] By contrast, one might well wonder about the reasons that impelled Vernant to formulate his thesis in terms that grant an undeniable *priority* to the political over the rational. It seems to me that we can find two.

The first reason is related to the fact that, while Vernant's analysis is principally guided by the epistemological problem of the Greek miracle, which sets in motion a return all the way back to the Mycenean origins (in virtue of the principle *nihil ex nihilo*), it remains simultaneously driven by its axiological dimension (in a relation that is never rendered truly explicit): the question here is not, moving back into the past, how to conceive the discontinuity of Greek thought (and of the city) with regard to what preceded them and what they emerged from, but rather, moving forward into the future, how to prevent the establishment of a fictive continuity and proximity between them and us, be this under the aegis of a paradigmatic Classicism, of a naïve nostalgia, of a sentimental consciousness, or of any other configuration derived from the Quarrel of the Ancients and the Moderns. In such a perspective, refusing the miracle means parting with the idea that there was a substantial continuity from them to us (which evidently does not mean that there was not a historical continuity) and distrusting any attempt at what one scholar has called an assimilation in the sense of "digestion."[37] The Greeks are one people like any other, without a particular privilege. And because the Greeks are like everyone, they are also different, different from others of course, but also and above all different from us. It is within such a perspective that Vernant always insisted on the fact that the Greeks' reason is not *our* reason, a reason that he characterizes, traditionally, as being scientific, experimental, and directed toward the mathematization and domination of nature. As for Greek reason, on his view it was "political," as it was not "so much the product of human commerce with things as of the relations of human beings with one another."[38] It can easily be understood that the genealogical model was at work here, with the mother city setting its seal, as it were, on its alleged daughter, reason, and then indirectly on her scions: that is the meaning of the "political" interpretation of Anaximander in the final chapter of *The Origins of Greek Thought*, in which Anaximander's cosmos, organized circularly around the center that is the earth, situated equidistantly from the borders, and staying in its place from the very fact of this equidistance, corresponds to the political geometry of the city, in which the decisions are taken "in the center."[39]

Is this characterization of Greek reason as political reason plausible in itself? One might well doubt it. For starting with its earliest manifestations, Greek rationality presents features, as for example a tendency toward systematization and rationalization (in the meaning of this term in Max Weber, who saw in this the distinctive feature of Western rationality[40]), that have nothing intrinsically political about them (which evidently does not mean that it might not directly or indirectly concern the sphere of politics). Hesiod's theological systematization, to take a particularly striking example, can hardly be conceived, *as systematization*, under the category of the political (without this at all excluding that its theme could be "political," as is indeed the case). Even if one were to grant to Vernant that Greek reason was never experimental, it seems difficult to deny that it made itself "theoretical" early enough in a sense that cannot be covered by the term "political."

But "political" can also be understood differently, as referring not to an intrinsic determination of reason but to the formal framework of its exercise. In this sense, Greek reason would be a daughter of the city in that it is within the public space of the city that rationality found a possibility for deploying its argumentative structures. To tell the truth, this idea too, as Vernant presents it, raises some questions. First, because one could easily maintain that the space in which rational thought was deployed was not only political but also antipolitical and transpolitical. Antipolitical, because the differentiation of the discipline of philosophy, and thus its specialization, leads to the formation of a class of experts who, so far from recognizing themselves within the public space, tend ostentatiously to separate themselves from it.[41] Heraclitus would doubtless be the best paradigm for this separation, but in fact it is ubiquitous. When Empedocles sings his *Purifications* at Olympia, his operation becomes meaningful only by opposition to the basic esotericism of the doctrine of his poem on nature, which is addressed to a single disciple. As for the transpolitical dimension of the development of rationality, this is connected with the phenomenon of Panhellenism, of which Olympia is precisely the symbol, that is, with a tendency toward universalization that transcends the framework of the city from the very moment that it is constituted.[42] On a more theoretical level, which takes us back to the Weberian problematic of causality in history, it would also be necessary to ask to what extent the city, considered as a formal framework, can be a *determining* factor, as is suggested by the formula of filiation ("rational thought, daughter of the city"). For whereas it seems hard to deny that the practice of judicial and political debate within the framework of the institutions of the democratic city *favored* the awareness of alternatives and the culture of discussion and rejoinder, one could maintain the idea, following J. Burckhardt, that it is instead the *agôn* or competition that is at the origin of the development of philosophy, as of other manifestations of Greek culture,[43] and this in turn would refer to something anterior to the city. Besides, it is not certain that contradictory debate weighed more in the emergence of philosophical discourse than the Homeric and Hesiodic truth claims, or indeed than the spread of writing.[44]

Beyond the objections that can be made to each of these two justifications for the primacy of the political, and the improvements or nuances that could be added appropriately according to the various cases, the principal problem that they present is that they do not easily cohabitate with one another. The procedural or formal conception of the relation between "city" and "rationality" means going beyond a perspective that aims—in virtue of the principle of transversal analogy—to discover the traces left behind by political *representations* within philosophical systems. It is perfectly compatible with the idea that Greek reason was capable of being theoretical, indeed experimental, if it ever had to be. One can even suggest that it is to the degree that Vernant was guided by a problematic of the "political" alterity of Greek reason that he was led to underestimate the principal effect of the solidarity between the discovery of the political space and the emergence of rationality to which he himself had drawn attention.

For it suffices to consider the implications of the procedural (or agonistic) perspective, and in particular the forms of intellectual radicalization that it made possible, to perceive that neither the category of positivity (naturalization or secularization) nor that of publicity makes it possible to give an account of the specific development of "philosophical" thought. But it is of this specificity, which is necessarily bound up with determinate contents, that an account must be given, if only so as not to sacrifice the "specific elaborations" to the generality of a phrase that puts an end to the Greek miracle but only at the price of an evident underdetermination.

The recourse to the Weberian model turns out to be useful here, less for its theory of the genesis of capitalist rationality from Calvinist ethics (for its mechanism is too specific to be applicable) than for the concept of rationality it employs.

Weber's project aims to understand why and how rationality took the distinctive form that it possesses within modern Western civilization, even though processes of rationalization are also at work in other great civilizations—this is why his studies on the great religions (Confucianism, Buddhism, Hinduism, Judaism, Islam) are the indispensable complement to *The Protestant Ethic and the Spirit of Capitalism* (*Die protestantische Ethik und der Geist des Kapitalismus*).[45] Weber's "Preliminary remark" (*Vorbemerkung*) to this latter book enumerates what he considers to be the principal expressions of Western rationalism. (In the summary that follows, I indicate with square brackets the feature that justifies the qualification of "rational" when the indication can be derived from Weber's text.) According to Weber, only the West has developed a rational science [i.e., mathematized]; a rational geometry [i.e., founded on proof]; rational natural sciences [i.e., experimental]; a rational chemistry [as opposed to alchemy]; a rational history [i.e., claiming a supratemporal validity]; a rational politics [i.e., of a systematic nature]; a rational law [i.e., systematically codified]; a rational artistic technique [i.e., with a mathematized and systematized harmony and compositional technique in music, a nondecorative, functional use of the Gothic arch in architecture, and a rational use of linear and atmospheric perspective in painting]; a rational organization of the transmission of knowledge [i.e., with the development of specialization]; the constitution of a rational administration [i.e., specialized] by functionaries of the state; a rational state [i.e., resting on a constitution]; and naturally a rational economy [i.e., under the aegis of capitalism].[46]

As this enumeration shows, Greek Western rationalism plays a nonnegligible role in the constitution of Western rationalism in general. Weber refers to "Hellenic rationalism" as a phenomenon that encompasses a number of disciplines, including mathematics (this must to begin with be Euclid's), history (Thucydides), and political theory (Aristotle). He pays homage to it in other texts, notably in the celebrated passage of the *Protestant Ethic* in which he

mentions Greek rationalism next to Jewish rationalism as one of
the two direct sources of Calvinist rationalism: "That great historic
process in the development of religions, the elimination of magic
from the world which had begun with the old Hebrew prophets
and, in conjunction with Hellenistic scientific thought, had repudi-
ated all magical means to salvation as superstition and sin, came
here [i.e., with the 'complete elimination of salvation through the
Church and the sacraments'] to its logical conclusion."[47] His study
of Confucianism and Taoism sometimes refers to Hellenic phenomena for the purpose of comparison. But these passages merely
render more tangible the fact that Weber never discussed Greek
rationalism *for itself*—something that is at first sight all the odder,
as Weber is explicitly engaged in a comparative project. The reference to Greece, present though it is, is always subordinate and never
takes on a *systematic* value.

But in fact this absence is logical, given that what specifically interests Weber is the relation existing between the phenomenon of
"rationalization" and the "great religions." His book *Economic Ethics
of the World Religions* (*Die Wirtschaftethik der Weltreligionen*) only
considers "the five systems of regulation of religious life or those
conditioned by religion that have been able to gather around themselves particularly large *masses* of the faithful: Confucian, Hindu,
Buddhist, Christian, Islamic religious ethics."[48] Judaism is added
because of the decisive role it played in both the formation of Christianity and in the development of Western capitalism. If Greek
polytheism is not part of this group of six, that is first of all because
it does not satisfy the criterion of the *mass*, which Weber considers
primary—a criterion that seems all the less applicable to Greek civilization, as this latter has died (this is not the case for any of the
other civilizations endowed with a "world religion"); the fact that
mainstream Greek polytheism does not include a soteriological dimension must also have played a role (Weber always speaks of religion in terms of a soteriology, *Heilslehre*). The two reasons combine
with one another and reinforce each other: for Weber, what determines the differentiated development of rationalisms is the *social*
weight of a determinate economic ethics (*Wirtschaftsethik*), and more
generally that of a way of life (*Lebensführung*)—a weight that only a

system of religious, and more precisely eschatological, beliefs is capable of guaranteeing. If restricted groups of experts (the "virtuosi") play an essential role in Weber's analysis, it is to the degree that they are the "bearers" of models that have an effective social resonance. But even if Greek rationalism was indeed the business of experts and implied, at least according to current representations, a certain way of life (the so-called theoretical one), it was also essentially extrareligious (which naturally does not prevent it from having had intrareligious effects) as well as being devoid of any solid sociological basis. This weakness can be considered as the counterpart of the extraordinary "acceleration" that characterizes the development of Greek philosophy between the sixth and fifth centuries BC—an acceleration that cannot be separated from a process of individualization marked, to stay with the case of philosophy, not only by the dense succession of new "visions of the world" proposed by a series of "I's" affirming themselves as such, but also by a *process of differentiation*, both external and internal, which defines new domains or "spheres" of competence—a process that also sealed the loss of the philosophers' political influence.[49]

If the role Greece plays in Weber's analysis is smaller than might have been expected, considering the importance he assigns it in the formation of modern rationalism, the set of conceptual tools he applies to the analysis of the processes of rationalization, Western or not, makes it possible to reflect on the case of the emergence of rationality in Greece in terms different from the ones that Vernant has proposed. For it rests upon a more complex concept of rationality, even if it too for its part is exposed to the accusation of being incomplete, insofar as one of Weber's fundamental theses is that ultimate values cannot become the object of a rational discussion.

It is notoriously difficult to establish a systematic typology of the forms of rationality in Weber. Weber refers sometimes to a "logical" or "theoretical-intellectual" rationality whose motor is "coherence" and the principle of "non-contradiction," and which he distinguishes from a "teleological" or "ethical-practical" rationality.[50] This distinction makes it possible to group together to a certain extent the different manifestations typical of Western rationality that were enumerated above: law, politics, and capitalism would essentially be functions of a teleological rationality, while the mathematical sciences, music, and painting would refer instead to a rationality of a logical type. One might hesitate in certain cases, for example architecture (where both aspects are present in equal measure) or printing. Three fundamental meanings of rationality have also been detected in Weber: a scientific-technical meaning, expressed by the development of instruments designed to control the world by means of calculation; a metaphysical-ethical meaning, expressed by the systematization of "meaning patterns," corresponding to what Weber calls "images of the world"; and a practical meaning, expressed by the adoption of a methodically regulated way of life.[51] Greek rationalism is evidently concerned in these three aspects, and already in its very first manifestations (making allowances for the necessary nuances). Even if Greek science never really engaged itself in technology or experimentation, it nonetheless made a decisive contribution to the formation of scientific rationalism (something that Weber too recognizes, as we have seen); Hellenic rationalism presents one of the clearest—and also one of the best known—cases of rationalism of images of the world, and the formula that Weber uses to characterize religious rationalism in relation to the problem of suffering and injustice ("integration within a pragmatic of universal, cosmic salvation") finds echoes in Presocratic philosophical rationalism as well, even if it certainly does not characterize the whole of it.[52] The "way of life," finally, is without any doubt a central category of Greek philosophy.

Weber builds a bridge between these different dimensions of rationality, because he is trying to identify the role, for the emergence of *capitalism* (the calculated organization of profit), of a certain *way of life* (practical aspect) and of the diffusion of a way of thinking that comes from a *religious ethic*, that is, from a determinate image of the world (Calvinism). It is within the framework of this complex problematic that one can explain the place Weber assigns to what he calls the "Ideas." For, as he says in a famous passage of the introduction to the *Economical Ethic of the World Religions*, "Not ideas, but material and ideal interests, directly govern men's conduct. Yet very frequently the 'world images' that have been created by 'ideas' have, like switchmen, determined the tracks along which action has been pushed by the dynamic of interest."[53] Recognizing the decisive character of the Ideas and of the "images of the world" within the process of rationalization, next to and in conjunction with more formal notions like those of "consequence" and "consistency," is indispensable for understanding the logic of the beginnings of Greek philosophy, because the intellectual differentiation that accompanies it is marked by a very high degree of heterogeneity— what Vernant's idea of political reason makes it impossible to explain, at least if this is understood substantially. For what the Presocratic philosophers confront us with is a conflictual diversity of images of the world, in relation to which the reader is invited to situate himself, and which transcend the categories of the city in every direction.

It would go beyond the goals of this introduction, which considers the Presocratics only collectively, to explore these images of the world further or to analyze the nature of the conflicts they generate and thus to enter into the specifics of Greek philosophical rationality. Instead we must return to the nature of our relation with them insofar as they are situated at the origin of Western philosophy. This will be the object of the final two chapters.

CHAPTER 5

Origins — our relation to the Pre Socratics

THE TERM "BREAKTHROUGH" (IN GERMAN, *DURCHBRUCH*) WAS used by K. Jaspers in his *The Origin and Goal of History*, first published in German in 1949, to refer to the series of unprecedented political and cultural upheavals experienced by ancient Greece starting in the seventh century BC—upheavals that in 1962 J.-P. Vernant in his *Origins of Greek Thought* was to call a "mutation."[1] The two terms correspond to different logics. While "mutation" refers to the problematic of discontinuity in history,[2] "breakthrough" suggests a trajectory in a certain direction, something like progress or an achievement that was determinant for a given history and that in one way or another continues in its effects until the present day.[3] Thus Jaspers's term, in conformity with the title of his book, suggests a teleological and axiological dimension that is absent from "mutation."

Jaspers had emphasized—indeed, this was his point—that other "breakthroughs" had taken place besides the Greek breakthrough, more or less at the same time in other places, in India, in China, in Palestine, under radically different conditions and with completely disparate effects. On the scale of the historical *longue durée* (to use F. Braudel's term), such a synchronicity could be considered absolute: that is why he called the first millennium before the Christian era an "axial" age—an epithet that is less than fully transparent and for which Eric Weil suggested substituting "bifurcatory," to describe the moment in which the history of humanity starts to go off in a new direction.[4] Jaspers's idea has been challenged, first of all because his construction does not grant the place they deserve to the great civilizations of writing (the Sumerian-Akkadian and Egyptian civilizations, which go back to the third millenium),[5] but also and above all because of its teleological implications. This is the very approach that Jacob Burckhardt, writing against the use of teleology in history by the philosophers of history and closely linking the concern for origins with the position of an ending, had refused in his *On the Study of History* (*Über das Studium der Geschichte*):

> The philosophers of history view the past as an antithesis and preliminary stage on the way to us as to what is more developed. We view what repeats itself, what is constant and typical as being something that resonates in us and is understandable. Those others are afflicted with speculations about beginnings and hence should really also speak about the future. We can do without those doctrines about beginnings, and no doctrine of the ending should be required of us.[6]

However, it is not certain that a historian should do without any teleological presuppositions whatsoever, or even that he would be capable of doing so, at least, in Kantian terms, at a reflective and not at a determinant level.[7] With regard to the Greeks at any rate, it is evident that the relation that "we" have to "them" weighs heavily on what we are led to say about them. For the fact is that, whether we like it or not, we are bound to them by an originary relation— not less than, but entirely differently from, our relation to the Jewish tradition.[8]

No specific problematic follows from this observation, nor, even less, does the slightest obligation. For different options are available for dealing with this kind of "originary" relation. This is because of the polysemy of the notion of origin, with which one can associate quite different representations. An origin can be nothing more than a *starting point*, but it can also be a *principle* or *foundation*. These two poles are doubled in their turn, since the principle or foundation of a given phenomenon can be nothing more than a simple *cause* or can take the particular form of a *norm*, while from a genetic point of view the starting point can reside either in the *sources* from which the phenomenon has come or by which it is nourished, but which are exterior to it, or in the very *beginnings* of its manifestation, which are fundamentally homogeneous with it. It is easy to see that these different distinctions are a function of the importance that is granted respectively to the two dimensions, temporal and axiological, in which the term can be understood, on a scale extending between the two poles of "genesis," considered as a process immersed in time, and "principle," which tends to detach itself from chronological considerations. This can be schematized in the following way:

Origin

+   Temporalization   –

(1) Genesis   (2) Principle

(1a) Sources   (1b) Beginnings   (2a) Cause   (2b) Norm

It turns out that these rubrics, which concern the historian's discourse about origins, whatever the origins are he is speaking about (it can be those of Greek thought, but also those of Christianity or the Kabbalah), also concern the directive categories of Presocratic thought, which constitute the object at issue insofar as it is the origin of Greek philosophy. The work of the Milesian cosmologists, Anaximander and Anaximenes, in which most scholars generally recognize the first manifestations of the birth of "philosophy," just like that of the great theogonic narratives (especially Hesiod's *Theogony*) from which they separate themselves, is in fact characterized not only by a movement of return to the origins (the genealogy of the gods in Hesiod, that of the universe among the Milesians), but also by the fact that this return is marked by a certain tension between two possible meanings of the origin, chronological and ontological.[9] In Hesiod, Zeus, who belongs to the third generation of the gods after Ouranus and Cronus, acquires a kind of derivative anteriority (and thereby a legitimation) by being the first of the gods to be regurgitated by his father Cronus, even if in the symbolic form of a stone.[10] Pherecydes of Syros, who composed, probably a little earlier than Anaximander, a theogony in prose that Aristotle located halfway between mythology and natural philosophy, stated at the beginning of his treatise that Zeus (named Zas) had *always* been, just like Chronus (time) and Chthoniê (the earth).[11] The same configuration is found at a higher level of abstraction in Anaximander, who, according to a possible interpretation of an indication that goes back to Theophrastus, was the first to use the term *arkhê* ("beginning") in the sense of "principle":[12] for this principle (in the present case, the "unlimited") also turns out to be "at the beginning."[13]

The polysemy of the term "origins" and the loaded character of its implications explain why certain authors choose to avoid the term, preferring "beginnings." In a book programmatically entitled *Beginnings*, E. Saïd noted, for example, "Thus between the word *beginning* and the word *origin* lies a constantly changing system of meanings, most of them of course making first one then the other word convey greater priority, importance, explanatory power." "As consistently as possible," he continues, "I use beginning as having the more active meaning, and origin the more passive one: thus 'X is the origin of Y', while 'the beginning of A leads to B'. In due course I hope to show, however, how ideas about origins, because of their passivity, are put to uses I believe ought to be avoided."[14] Saïd is evidently thinking here of the ideological use of origins, which can all too easily debase historical research. In the case of Greece, M. Bernal's theses on the Egyptian (putatively "black") origin of the Greek breakthrough supply a sad example.[15] But Diogenes Laertius already provides evidence in the prologue of his *Lives of Eminent Philosophers* for the existence of a Hellenocentric reaction against the thesis, maintained by the Christian author Clement of Alexandria, that the Greeks had "stolen" their philosophy from the Bible.[16]

Within the framework of a critique of G. Scholem's theses regarding the origins of the Kabbalah, M. Idel has reformulated the distinction between beginnings and origins in the following terms:

> The former term represents not only a more active versus a more passive concept. In my opinion the concept of beginning reflects better an awareness of the historical moments when some idea, term or system are believed to have been innovated as well as the processes involved in this innovation. 'Origins', on the other hand, point to a certain resistance to focusing too strongly on finding a

specific point in time which generates a certain spiritual phenomena. This term takes in consideration more the sources of a certain phenomenon rather than the moment of its emergence.[17]

It is not enough for the historian to identify the "sources" of the Kabbalah, which as it happens are Gnosticism and Neoplatonism, according to Scholem, insofar as his task would be to give an account of the complex process of an emergence that obeys a historically observable chronology. But there is more, and it is more serious. To relegate to the background the processes of emergence favors the adoption of normative perspectives. It is not only because origins are insufficiently temporalized that they are insufficiently historical objects: they are also, and above all, intrinsically suspect. This is how, by attributing the origin of the Kabbalah to "a revolt, partly perhaps of Jewish origin, against anti-mythical Judaism," Scholem would have constructed a homology, itself mythical, between the Kabbalistic movement and the Zionist one, the two meeting in a shared reaction to a certain version of Jewish rationalism.[18] In this way, Scholem would himself deserve the title of "Gnostic," insofar as one essential feature of every Gnosticism resides in its refusal to separate the origins from the goal or end.[19] This is the same as saying that what is being betrayed is history itself, in whose name the Kabbalah had first been mobilized against its elimination in the "enlightened" tradition of Jewish history.

But nothing suggests that we gain very much if we speak of "beginnings" rather than of "origins." First, the semantic analyses that aim to distinguish between "origins" and "beginnings" can easily be reversed. For if it is true that in certain cases the historicity of beginnings can be played off against the normativity of origins, the term "origin" is itself far from being necessarily loaded with undesirable eschatological connotations. E. Renan, for example, for whom "a history of the *Origins of Christianity* would have to include all of the dark and … subterranean period that extends from the first beginnings of this religion until the moment when its existence becomes a public, notorious fact, one that is evident to everyone's eyes,"[20] evidently takes "origins" in a sense near to what M. Idel calls "beginnings." And to return to Greece, J.-P. Vernant's *Origins of Greek Thought* refers the "origins" not to "sources," but to a set of historical, cultural, and structural factors, whose interaction finally made the beginnings of Greek philosophy possible, but only at the end of a complex process. This is also why, to the reader's possible surprise, Vernant's book *concludes* with a chapter dedicated to Anaximander (who has often been used as a starting point) once he has reconstructed *ab origine* the process of the emergence of the city (itself the mother of the new Greek rationality, according to his thesis) following on the collapse of Mycenean royalty in the twelfth century BC. It is hard to imagine a stronger historicization and a greater temporalization of origins.

Inversely, *beginnings* are no less exposed to the influence of an unwelcome normativity than origins are. Perhaps, in a certain way, they are even more exposed to it. For a beginning tends to be *homogeneous* with what it is the beginning of, unlike the relation existing between the "origin" and the "originated" that issues from it, which not only is compatible with the heterogeneity of the two, but most often presupposes it (neither Gnosticism nor Neoplatonism is *already* the Kabbalah). What there is a beginning of already exists as such. To this degree, the notion of "beginning" leads just as much to investing the originary with extraneous concepts or problematics as that of "origin" does, when it does not lead to magnifying these ideologically. Heidegger's "originary thinkers," officially three in number (Anaximander, Parmenides, and Heraclitus), supply a clear illustration of this—those figures whose shared mythical function is to testify to the simultaneity of the "withdrawal" and "blooming" of Being through certain great privileged words of the Greek language (*phusis*, *logos*, or *alêtheia*).[21] An example of another kind is supplied by the mythic figure of the "first inventor" (*prôtos heuretês*), which is recurrent in Greek stories of origins.[22] If the stakes in identifying the first inventor are so high, this is because he determines the very form of the invention. This is as true for philosophy as it is for the other arts. In Aristotle's story about the beginnings of philosophy in the first book of his *Metaphysics*, he attributes to the "first philosophers," and in particular to Thales, the merit of having had for the first time the idea of a material principle that would be the "substrate" of all things and in which their "nature" would consist. But it is known (from Diogenes Laertius in particular) that some people claimed that this same concept went back to Musaeus, the disciple of Orpheus, manifestly in disagreement with the Aristotelian model and in rivalry with him about the question of philosophical priority.[23] For his part, Theophrastus, Aristotle's disciple and successor, maintained, on the basis of an interpretation of Thales's interests as being less metaphysical than astronomical, that Thales "had been preceded by many others" in the "inquiry on nature," whom he had succeeded in eclipsing only by virtue of his undeniable "superiority."[24] Others, using another kind of criterion, invoked Pythagoras as the inventor of philosophy: he is the one who allegedly introduced the very term "philosophy," defining it less by a theoretical *content* like the "substrate" than by its *form*—in this case, the adoption of a "theoretical" attitude that pursues knowledge for its own sake (which explains why the heavens are its privileged object).[25] The starting points can evidently be multiplied depending on how philosophy is defined. This is just as true for the modern historian as for the Ancients. Despite the immense influence exerted by Aristotle's narrative, which had the effect of exalting Thales to the rank of "the first philosopher," Anaximander and Parmenides, later than Thales, or again Pherecydes or indeed Hesiod, earlier than him, are just as strong potential candidates for the "invention" (be it even inchoate) of this embryonic discipline—if one really wishes to name candidates.[26]

We touch here on the historiographical question of what it is that "marks an epoch," that is, that interrupts one continuity, according to the etymological meaning of the term (the *epochê* is first of all a "suspension"), for the benefit of another one. The historical use of this category since the eighteenth century to characterize the entirety of a period that is inaugurated by a reference event (or, in the case of the Presocratics, concluded by one) can easily give rise to two paralogisms, which could be called the extensional paralogism of exhaustive subsumption, which transforms a characterization in terms of a tendency or an ideal type into an intrinsic determination of the period considered (in the case of Presocratic philosophy, the notion of "natural philosophy" has often played this role[27]), and the epistemological paralogism of the cause, which tends to neglect the symbolic function attributed to the event considered initial (or terminal, at the end of the period considered) in order to assign to it the efficacy of a real determination (for the period we are considering, it is essentially Thales and Socrates that are at issue here).

H. Blumenberg has demonstrated the dynamic of this second paralogism very clearly by showing how historical science, which earlier, in its Romantic phase, had been strongly based on the concept of epoch (which presented itself as a paradigm of historical individuality), was also constantly led to blur the limits of the concept in the very name of history, by multiplying the intermediary stages of the epochs and thereby gradually relativizing the importance of the caesuras between them.[28] In the course of these regressions, the epoch lost its vocation as an intrinsic and substantial determination, to become, according to Blumenberg, a methodical means of classification of doubtful reliability.[29]

In fact, what is mythic in this case is the act of tracing a unique line of demarcation and positing an absolute starting point, which tends, significantly, to take on a form that is calendric, when it is not astrological. The Battles of Valmy (1791) among the Moderns and of Salamis (480 BC) among the Ancients provide two eminent examples of this.[30] In the domain of the history of philosophy, the synchronism of the year 1642, in which Galileo died and Newton was born, also marks the limit between two epochs.[31] It was against this type of illusion that Blumenberg deployed the resources of temporal margins under the name of *limes*—literally, the buffer zone separating the Roman Empire from what was outside it. Historically, things have switched, without our ever being able to say exactly when.[32] Blumenberg's *limes* is, as it were, the name for all the historical complexities whose effect can be measured but whose precise demarcation cannot be determined. This is why Blumenberg substituted for a starting point that is unique and that should be considered fictive the consideration of two reference points, on one side and the other of a perspicuous transformation, that provide evidence for the reality of intervening changes: that is the meaning of his comparative analysis of Nicholas of Cusa's thought for what is earlier and of Giordano Bruno's for what is later.

The pertinence of this problematic for the analysis of the "beginnings of philosophy" is obvious: Thales (or someone else) is the functional equivalent of Valmy or the year 1642. The question is whether, in the analysis of the origins of Greek thought, one ought not, like Blumenberg, to substitute for the transparent but mythical fixity of starting points the more prudent model of "reference points" that are fixed on one side and the other of a large frontier whose outlines are fluid.

In an approach of this sort, there are certainly many advantages, and a great deal of truth. However, prudence, too, should not be employed imprudently. In his essay "The Form of the Concept in Mythic Thought" ("Die Begriffsform im mythischen Denken"), E. Cassirer noted with regard to the Renaissance that the possibility of designating "almost exactly the moment in which a 'revolution in the mode of thought' begins" is "a rare phenomenon in the history of thought and ideas."[33] "Almost" means almost, but "rare" implies possible. It is true that in Cassirer the starting point in question already presents a certain complexity, since what is involved is neither a unique event nor a unique name but a certain "convergence": according to him, the birth of modern scientific thought can be located at the conjuncture of two events, the publication of Descartes's *Rules for the Direction of the Mind* (composed around 1628), which formulates for the first time the idea of a *mathesis universalis* as an overarching science of measure, order, and number, and the late but irrevocable rejection by Kepler in his *Harmony of the World* of 1619 of the astrological mode of thought with which he had identified himself for a long time.[34] This remark, coming from a scholar conscious of the exceptional character of this constellation, inspires us to take a second look: the birth of philosophy in Greece is not an event whose nature is less epochal than the birth of modern science, and historical reason is nourished no less by discontinuities than by continuities.

In the case of Antiquity, the problem is complicated by the fact that, at least in certain cases, our information on some of the found-

ing figures is evidently (or almost evidently) the result of retroactive projections—thus the attribution to Thales of a doctrine of the substrate, or to Pythagoras of the neologism "philosophy." Complicated, not simplified: for neither can these constructions be simply *eliminated* in an offhand way. As we saw in an earlier chapter, the question certainly arises to what extent there might not be a certain historical truth in this filiation or that one, like the one linking Socrates to Archelaus (which there are good reasons to consider to be a construction).[35]

Beyond various contingent, essentially technical problems as well as methodological ones deriving from the state and nature of our sources, which require a certain lightness of touch in order to be evaluated and used, a more general problem is posed: that of the reference to individuals in the construction of historical epochs. Such a reference will seem all the more legitimate when dealing with an historical epoch in which the individual as author or creator was conceived as being differentiated (this is one of the aspects of the "mutation" of the seventh through sixth centuries BC in Greece)[36]— provided that one works with a demythified concept of "beginnings" or "origins." E. Saïd notes pertinently that beginnings are characterized less by the fact of being what they are than by what they make possible or "authorize."[37] The term is useful: it outlines a concept of beginning that is less heroic and more modest than that of the "first inventor," at the same time assigning a suitable place to the crucial events of the history of thought. In fact, such a concept of beginning could itself be "authorized" by two celebrated lines of Xenophanes, which state, "The gods have not indicated all things to mortals from the beginning [*ap' archês*], / But in time, by searching, they find something more that is better,"[38] or again by Aristotle, who points out the necessary difficulty of beginnings in the last chapter of his *Sophistic Refutations*, when he observes that he is the first person to have marked off the field of logical analysis (something that could not reasonably be denied).[39] It is true that this very precariousness implies a certain heterogeneity between the "beginnings" and what they are the beginnings of (just as was the case a little earlier for the origin)—this is an aspect that Aristotle does not, and surely could not, emphasize because of his ultimate metaphysical presuppositions.

Piecemeal progress does not mean the identity of a substance that passes gradually from potentiality to actuality so as to reveal a nature that was present from the beginning, as Aristotle thought not only in the case of natural movement, but also in the cases of historical movement in general and of the history of philosophy in particular,[40] but instead the emergence of projects that are capable of "authorizing themselves," and that in fact authorize themselves, by the other project that preceded them, so as to develop it, to inflect it, or to contest it in a new and unforeseeable direction. From this point of view, it is under the sign of Xenophanes, more even than under that of Aristotle, that we can place the study of the origins or beginnings (whichever term one prefers) of philosophy in Greece.

CHAPTER 6

What Is at Stake

[Handwritten annotations: "— Talcott doesn't like this chapter"; "• people interpret socratics through on philosophical perspective LAK A: thats okay B: We can do our own assesment through same system"]

CONSIDERED AS A CERTAIN GROUP OF THINKERS (RATHER THAN as the individual thinkers they also are), the Presocratics illustrate paradigmatically two possible ways of relating to origins, in the present case to the origins of Greek rationality: according to whether these are placed under the aegis of the other or of the same, under that of discontinuity or of continuity. The two ancient traditions that I distinguished in the first chapter under the names of Socratic-Ciceronian and Platonic-Aristotelian were divided precisely on this point.[1] They have their modern counterparts in an antirationalist tradition, which prolongs Nietzsche's revaluation and contests any continuist historiography of an Aristotelian type in the name of a certain otherness, and a rationalist current, which identifies problems posited by the Presocratics from which the posterity of philosophy will never cease to draw nourishment. How these two options are specified varies as a function of knowledge interests (to adopt Habermas's term) and of the philosophical tradition, giving rise to potentially or actually competing models that this introduction cannot aim to analyze in their particularity. If I choose to illustrate this point by reference to two authors from the German tradition, E. Cassirer and H.-G. Gadamer, it is because I am relatively familiar with them, but the *general* point that my characterization of their respective approaches is intended to illustrate concerns just as much the Anglo-Saxon historiography of ancient philosophy as the positions belonging to the perspective considered "Continental."

There can be no doubt that it is phenomenology that offers the most philosophically and historiographically influential modern version of a discontinuist model. This position can be conveniently

[Handwritten annotation in left margin: "Lak & him"]

illustrated, rather than by reference to Heidegger himself (who would require an independent analysis), by Gadamer's introductory lectures on *The Beginning of Philosophy*,[2] which collect the substance of articles he dedicated to this subject starting in the 1930s and which reflect the fundamental tendencies of the Heideggerian approach. Two convictions guide Gadamer's analysis. The former leads him to maintain that it is only Parmenides who really counts in Presocratic philosophy—a thesis whose pedigree reaches back to Plato's *Sophist*, where Parmenides was promoted to the status of "father."[3] It is only in relation to him that the other philosophers, including Heraclitus, can be interpreted. The latter conviction, of a methodological order, has to do with two of the characteristics that distinguish the Presocratics. First, they are located at a beginning— in the present case, the beginning of Greek philosophy (the subtitle of the *Lectures* is less restrictive: what they consider is simply philosophy). And second, their works are transmitted only indirectly, by summaries and quotations, and thus in a filtered and fragmentary manner. These two features allow Gadamer to situate his approach with regard to two theories of history that appear to be opposed but whose complicity he denounces, those of Hegel (taken as representative of historical teleology) and of scientistic historicism (represented in particular by H. Diels). These two formal determinations— beginning and fragmentation—lead back to Parmenides as the central figure of Presocratic philosophy, given that Parmenides not only inaugurates philosophy in the proper sense but also that he is the only one who can be read to a certain extent "for himself," in a text that, by an oxymoron, could be called partially complete.[4]

On the teleological front, Gadamer develops a simple argument with which it is hard to disagree: he frees the concept of beginning from the influence of evolutionism. His idea is that the notion of development implies a series of necessary stages, all of them included in the origin from the beginning, that go all the way until they reach a determinate endpoint, in such a way that the *telos* already exists in potential in the seed. Instead of the metaphor of potentiality and germination, Gadamer prefers that of a *youth* of philosophy, youth being understood as the period of at least a multiplicity of possibilities, if not of the totality of all possibilities whatsoever.[5]

In itself, this metaphor, with the idea of opening it implies, is perfectly acceptable. But it becomes problematic in the way Gadamer uses it. First of all, there is the question whether Gadamer really escapes from the dialectic of the conceptual pair beginning/ end, indeed whether he can even wish really to escape from it, considering the very principles of his hermeneutics, which rests upon the idea that understanding a text depends upon the "fusion of horizons" of the author and his interpreter. He himself notes that "the beginning always implies the end,"[6] and when he speaks of the prehistory (*Vorgeschichte*) of metaphysics or entitles one section of his work "On the Way to Plato" (*Auf dem Wege zu Platon*),[7] he gives the impression that Plato completes what Parmenides began.

Second, and above all, there is the question to what extent the analyses he proposes succeed in giving a plausible image of this "youth." For Gadamer's approach is strongly marked by his desire to minimize, indeed to deny, the role of discussion, criticism, and polemic within Presocratic thought—something that not only fits badly with the idea one might legitimately have about youth but that is also eminently contestable in itself. This thesis, which he takes over practically unchanged from Heidegger,[8] goes along with a revision of the traditional relation postulated between Parmenides and Heraclitus: the one is not responding to the other, as the fundamental scheme of the Hegelian dialectic supposes, whoever is thought to be responding to whom, whether Heraclitus to Parmenides (as in Hegel, where the moment of becoming follows that of being), or Parmenides to Heraclitus (according to a view that has been widely shared since Jacob Bernays). On the contrary, the two philosophers' thoughts are here taken to be independent of one another. Gadamer often insists on the liberation afforded, from this point of view as from others, by K. Reinhardt's book *Parmenides and the History of Philosophy* (*Parmenides und die Geschichte der Philosophie*), which appeared in 1916. For it was Reinhardt's merit to maintain that Parmenides's Fragment 28B6 DK (= Frag D7 LM), with its attack against "two-headed" mortals who live in the double perspective of nonbeing as well as of being, is directed not against Heraclitus but instead against humans in general.[9] This argument, which refuses to identify mortals with Heraclitus (but this would hold for any other philosopher too), is in fact not really compelling, for it is not clear why the "opinions of mortals" would not include the opinions of philosophers, who, from the point of view of Parmenides and his goddess, merely articulate the *implicit* position of mortals (this question, which is interesting from a hermeneutic point of view, would require a detailed discussion). But even if Reinhardt were right on this point, it is the generalization to which Gadamer proceeds on the basis of this particular case that remains implausible, or more precisely the fact that he considers this particular case to be the illustration of a general rule: if Parmenides does not attack Heraclitus, it is because the Presocratics do not respond to one another. Gadamer thus opposes what he calls the *interpretatio hegeliana*, a phrase that covers not only the official Hegelianism of Hegel's philosophy of history but also the rampant Hegelianism that Gadamer sees at work in the ordinary and least Hegelian historians of ancient philosophy (to say nothing of Zeller, in whom Hegel's influence is not only patent but is also explicitly asserted[10]):

> ... we must refuse to believe not only the *interpretatio aristotelica*, which provides the basis for Theophrastus and the doxographers, but so too also the *interpretatio* that dominates the whole historical and philological thought of modernity—despite the anti-Hegelianism of the historical school—and that I would like to call the *interpretatio hegeliana*. Its presupposition, taken as being self-evident, is, to be sure, not, as in Hegel, the total comprehensibility of history on the basis of its inner "logic"—but for it too it is certain that the individual thinkers and their doctrines are related to one another, "overtake," criticize, fight one another, so that a logically understandable coherence organizes the dialogue of tradition.[11]

Thus the conception of Presocratic philosophy we find here could well be called not only antidialectical but even antirelational. At first sight, this conception might seem odd in the context of Gadamer's self-professed dialogism. But in fact it perfectly reflects the existence of an inherent tension between two philosophical models in Gadamer himself—that of historiality (the Presocratics as a phase in the history of being) and that of dialogue (represented in a certain way by the Platonic moment)—but also, and doubtless more precisely, a conception of dialogue that is devoid of any genuinely dialogical character (this explains how Gadamer can read Plato in the light of the Presocratics).[12] The positive counterpart of this antirelational interpretation is not, as in Nietzsche's conception, a theory of grand individuals, of those "tyrants of the spirit" each of whom "possessed a sturdy belief in himself and in his 'truth' and with this overthrew all their neighbors and predecessors,"[13] but a fundamentally homogenizing approach in virtue of which the first thinkers of Greece all speak with a single voice. To be sure, there is a difference between the Ionians and Parmenides: the former think about *phusis*, the latter about an immediate apprehension of what is (in conformity with an untraditional but distinctive interpretation on the part of the phenomenological tradition).[14] But in truth the former is connected with the latter by an uninterrupted continuity. Parmenides is, as it were, the truth of the Ionians:

> For the result is an astonishing uniformity in its basic motif for all the Presocratic philosophy of the first period. The Milesians, Parmenides, and Heraclitus express the same basic view of the unity of difference. I see nothing strange in this result. On the contrary: we must learn to free ourselves not only from the Aristotelian idea, but also from the Hegelian and modern one, that these thinkers form a connected sequence. They do not ever philosophize against one another but instead as philosophers against the non-philosophy of mortals.[15]

In the case of the Presocratics, the overcoming of historicism invokes Plato, who is there to indicate the outlines of the unity of Ionian thought, indeed of that of the whole of Presocratic thought. For Gadamer suggests, not without some artifice, that the opposition between the Eleatics and the other Presocratic thinkers, whom Plato collects together under the name of Heracliteans in the *Theaetetus*,[16] results from the particular interest Plato was able to find in the Eleatic doctrine of being. It does not affect the deeper unity that joins them together.

It is above all the way in which Plato sees his "predecessors" that facilitates this task. For he saw them all—with the sole exception of the Eleatics—as a unity and he baptized them all with a single name by calling them "Heracliteans." It is obvious that this way of conceiving of the tradition is an antithetical construction, that its genuine motivation is the positive reception of the Eleatic idea of being by means of the theory of Ideas. In this way the history of the reception of Eleatic thought will always provide an essential access to the Eleatic doctrine, and Plato is located at its summit.[17]

In his concentration on Plato, taken as "an incomparable witness for the beginnings of philosophy,"[18] Gadamer returns *mutatis mutandis* to the gesture of Hegel, who defends Aristotle as a perfectly sufficient source for knowledge of the beginnings of philosophy.[19] Gadamer is also led to minimize the information Aristotle provides in the first book of the *Metaphysics*, where discussion, polemic, argument, and progress form the center of an exposition that is strongly marked by a teleological conception of history—everything that Gadamer calls the *interpretatio hegeliana* being already present in Aristotle.[20] It remains disquieting that *Wirkungsgeschichte*,[21] which is indeed at work here, seems in the end to come to terms very well indeed with the loss of the original works—one has the impression that these would say nothing more than what Plato says about them. This is a new tension within Gadamer's position: between this very principle and the recognition that a direct access to the complete works, one unmediated by Plato and Aristotle, is essential for understanding them.[22]

Although Gadamer does not cite Cassirer in this context,[23] the way in which the latter discusses the Presocratics supplies a perfect example of the kind of history that Gadamer condemns. It is worthwhile to consider Cassirer's approach, not only because it is not known well enough, but also because, despite the objections to which it is exposed (including those that Gadamer articulates against any historiography of a Hegelian type) and despite the outdatedness of some of its interpretations, it possesses an informational quality and a philosophical pertinence far superior to what can be derived from reading Gadamer. It might even be suggested that Cassirer's exposition still constitutes one of the best available introductions to Presocratic philosophy.

All of Cassirer's writings, even the most systematic ones, have a significant historical dimension that articulates, with different degrees of generality and temporal scale, a number of sequences belonging to the history of philosophy, the sciences, and thought in general, given that Cassirer does not separate the history of philosophy from intellectual history. Antiquity has always played an important role in these sequences, both before and after the publication in 1910 of Cassirer's *Substance and Function*, which marks an important shift in his interpretation of the large-scale relation between Antiquity and Modernity. For in the chapter dedicated to ancient thought that serves as an introduction to the first volume of *The Problem of Knowledge*, published in 1906,[24] Cassirer still presupposed that a fundamental continuity linked ancient thought and modern thought, insofar as he considered that the "internal progress" of modern thought, which has led it to set the problem of knowledge at the heart of its concerns rather than subordinating it to other systematic questions, went back to the principles of Greek thought, in the present case identified with the Platonic theory of scientific knowledge in H. Cohen and P. Natorp's Neokantian version of it.[25] It is this continuity that is put into question by Cassirer's new distinction between substance and function, which will henceforth serve as a way of distinguishing Antiquity from Modernity: whereas ancient thought was essentially substantial (this puts into question the Neokantians' de-substantializing interpretation of the Platonic theory of Ideas), modern thought is essentially functional (relational). This explains why Cassirer did not reprint the 1906 chapter in the second edition of *The Problem of Knowledge*.[26]

Nevertheless, Cassirer remained very interested in the genesis and development of Greek philosophy. Toward the end of his life, he takes the emergence of Greek thought, understood broadly, as the object of his article "*Logos, Dike, Kosmos*," which appeared in Sweden in 1941. That same year, Cassirer taught a course at Yale on the history of ancient philosophy that contains a series of lectures on the first philosophers.[27] But his most concentrated and systematic text on this subject is constituted by the first section, entitled "The Philosophy of the Greeks from the Beginnings to Plato" ("Die Philosophie der Griechen von den Anfängen bis Platon"), which opens the first volume, dedicated to the history of philosophy, of the *Manual of Philosophy* (*Lehrbuch der Philosophie*) that was published by Max Dessoir in 1925.[28]

Cassirer follows the first book of Aristotle's *Metaphysics* when he discusses the beginnings of Greek philosophy up to and including Plato, as for his part J. Burnet had done in a classic history of philosophy "from Thales to Plato" published in 1914.[29] Cassirer's choice doubtless reflects his wish to distance himself from the post-Nietzschean way of looking at the Presocratics that was dominant in Germany during the 1920s.[30] Within the pre-Aristotelian group, Cassirer adopts a purely geographic and hence conceptually neutral division between "pre-Attic philosophy" (*Vorattische Philosophie*) and "Attic philosophy" (*Attische philosophie*).[31] Nonetheless, he maintains the distinction between an earlier orientation of philosophy toward "nature" and a sequel in Socrates and Plato that takes the measure of man and subjectivity and opens out onto a philosophy of a *semantic* inspiration. For Cassirer offers an original interpretation that breaks with the Neokantians' purely epistemological approach and instead seeks predecessors within the history of the antecedents of the philosophy of symbolic forms (of which Cassirer's elaboration was contemporary with his composition of this chapter), and by doing so he conceives of the transition from the Presocratics to Plato as being one from "the Being of things as they are given in space or time" to "the Being of meanings."[32]

Cassirer places the whole of history under the sign of a development (*Entwicklung*) that is characterized, according to a phrase that evidently is profoundly inspired by Hegel, as the "history of the self-discovery of the *logos*" (*Geschichte des sich selbst Findens des Logos*)—a discovery that comprises three stages: knowledge of nature, moral knowledge, and knowledge of knowledge.[33]

Within "pre-Attic philosophy," the only one that concerns us here, Cassirer distinguishes four systematically linked stages that correspond in fact to three grand moments (since the first two stages merely represent two complementary aspects of one and the same position):

(1) Ionian philosophy (i.e., Anaximander and Anaximenes), which answers the question "from what?" (*woher?*) and considers things in their beginning (*Anfang*), still speaks the mythic *language* of the origin (*Ursprung*); but in fact it discovers the identity of *phusis*, and thus virtually the category of substance or *ousia*, through the very form of its questioning, if not in a conceptually articulated manner.[34] However, there is a "dialectical tension" between the two contradictory demands of universality (which Anaximander has the role of representing) and immanence (this is Anaximenes's role).[35] In order to overcome the myth and its particular embeddedness and attain the universality of a principle, Anaximander had in effect to pay the price of its transcendence: his principle, the unlimited (*apeiron*), is located beyond all the determinations that are immanent in the world. Paradoxically, he thus preserves the trace of the myth that he contributes to overcoming. Inversely, Anaximenes, by restoring the principle to immanence (this is what is meant by his choice of air, after Anaximander's unlimited), also sacrifices the universality that guaranteed the abstraction of Anaximander's principle. Thereafter the shared task of Heraclitus and Pythagoras will be to conceive the universality of the principle conjointly with its immanence.

(2) This is the function assigned to the first thematization of the *logos*, in the form of measure (in Pythagoras) and harmony (in Heraclitus). This movement away from the problem of genesis also amounts to a process of desubstantialization (thus, the passage from substance to function is in some sense already at work at the very beginning of Greek thought). The guiding notion is no longer "provenance" (*Entstehung*) but "state" (*Bestand*); attention is directed no longer toward matter (*Stoff*) but toward structure (conceived in the case of Heraclitus as the "tension of contraries," *Spannung der Gegensätze*),[36] the ways in which processes are regulated, and form (Cassirer himself speaks with regard to the *logos* of a "relational concept," *Verhältnisbegriff*[37]). The duality Heraclitus-Pythagoras gives rise to a dialectic that is analogous, at another level, to that of the pair Anaximander-Anaximenes. Heraclitus certainly thinks in terms of a form, but in a manner that is general, intuitive, imagistic; for its

part, Pythagorean number is specific, scientific, abstract, and it opens up the possibility of an experimental knowledge that Heraclitus's powerful but general insight does not authorize. Pythagoras, a man of science, is the man of theory, in conformity with the ancient tradition.[38] It is with him that the category of "truth" begins to emerge, even if only as an "intermediary concept between the being of things and number."[39] The anchoring of truth in the *logos*, and as a consequence the discovery of the *logos* in the proper sense, is reserved for Eleatism.

[margin note: logos as truth consummated by Eleatics]

(3) Eleatism (Xenophanes and Parmenides). Xenophanes forms a kind of transition between the group of earlier thinkers and Parmenides, insofar as his problematic, which "does not directly concern nature" but being, nonetheless bears not on being in general but on the being of the divine.[40] All the same, it leads to Parmenides's "panlogism" (*Panlogismus*).[41] For Parmenides proceeds in the first part of his poem to destroy the categories that underlie physics, with the affirmation of the principle of the identity of being to itself, which constitutes the birthdate of the logic of identity $(A=A)$.[42] The second part of the poem claims to develop a "physics" just as little as the first part did. It is directed not toward the object, even if this is "natural" in the present case, but toward the conditions of possibility of the error that this very physics constitutes, in perfect agreement with the principles developed in the first part: one should intepret it not as "a doctrine of *phusis*, but a doctrine of physics."[43] If the guiding concept remains that of truth, this latter is no longer the object of a response that is quantitative and objective (though purely formal), as in Pythagoras: the question is not that of knowing "how much," but "whether (it is the case)."[44] The problem is that of the possibility of inquiry and of the path (*hodos*) that this latter must follow. Thus Parmenides is defined as "the first methodologist" (*der erste Methodiker*). The refusal of physics for the benefit of an onto*logy* that is first of all logical has a first positive counterpart, claimed as such by Parmenides. This is the correlation between thought and being, under whose aegis Cassirer places not only Parmenides himself but the whole initial phase of Greek philosophy: for it is a general characteristic of pre-Attic (i.e., presemantic) philosophy to discover, simultaneously and by one and the same move-

ment, the world *and* the thought that grasps it.[45] It is this moment of correspondence, implicit in his predecessors' approach just as in his successors', that Parmenides states explicitly when he affirms the essential solidarity (if not the identity) between thought and being.[46] This profound agreement between the pre- and post-Parmenidean natural philosophers and their most radical critic, though paradoxical at first glance, is manifested even more clearly by what can legitimately be described as a historical "ruse of reason." For by destroying earlier physics, Parmenides objectively prepares the terrain for the new natural philosophy—the third one after the "substantialists" (Ionians) and the "structuralists" (Heraclitus/Pythagoras):[47] this will be the renewal of the philosophy of nature among the post-Parmenideans (the *Jüngere Naturphilosophie*), which in Cassirer's perspective is also the first philosophy of nature in the proper sense of the term to merit this name, since it rests upon the category of "foundation" (*Grund*) or *principle of reason*.

(4) The last stage of the self-discovery of the *logos* in its pre-Attic phase consists in the thematization of the "foundation" in the form of the principle of reason, understood as a reconciliation between the two first phases (which are objective and revolve around reality), on the one hand, and the third one (logical and revolving around the truth) that preceded it (this is why the quadripartition in fact stands in for a tripartition), on the other. After the Parmenidean destruction of physics, this is a matter of rediscovering a "physiology," understood in the strict sense as "the thought of a harmony between *logos* and *phusis*."[48] This construction rests upon an extension to Anaxagoras and Empedocles of Aristotle's interpretation of Leucippus as having sought to reconcile Parmenidean ontology with sensory reality.[49] What is involved is "saving the world of appearances."[50] Cassirer locates the analysis at the epistemological level to begin with: among these three thinkers there is a collaboration between reason and the senses.[51] This perspective can certainly be explained in part by Cassirer's concern to attribute to Anaxagoras and Empedocles a level of reflection equal to that of Parmenides.[52] More profoundly, one can also see in it a consequence of the semantic turn he gives to the interpretation of Plato, with pre-Attic philosophy already taking charge in this way of the reconciliation between truth

and logic that the Neokantians had considered to be the ambition distinctive of Platonic thought.

Cassirer distinguishes three substages in the articulation of the category of foundation, represented by Empedocles, Anaxagoras, and Leucippus, respectively. At the conclusion of this movement, the Eleatics' analytic logic, which knows only the unity of the identical, is replaced by the synthetic logic of the Atomists' aetiology (or the search for causes, *aitiologia*), which posits the unity of the different. In opposition to Parmenides, the separation between the foundation and what is founded (*Grund/Gegründete*) is concretized in a series of innovations all going in the direction of a theory of superior knowledge: a new concept of the phenomenon (in the sense of "what appears," *Erscheinung*) makes it possible to put an end to the "Ionian" oscillation between two interpretations of the principle (as foundation, *Grund*, and as beginning, *Anfang*); a distinction between two levels of reflection makes it possible to resolve the question of the principle's immanence or nonimmanence; and the substitution of the requirement of analysis (*Forderung der Analyse*) for the "intuition of nature" (*Anschauung der Natur*) opens the way for the reduction to the elements, which in Leucippus take on the classic form of atomic elements (*stoikheia*), in Anaxagoras that of "seeds" (*spermata*), and in Empedocles that of "roots" (*rhizômata*).

In each of these three cases, the operation of the principle of reason presents itself in particular forms, regardless of whether what is involved is the nature of the elements or the relation that is supposed to exist among them. Within the perspective of the principle of reason, the adequation between the specific determination of what the element is and the function that belongs to it increases from Empedocles to Leucippus. Empedocles's elements are nothing more than a simple hypostasis of sensory data. Anaxagoras's doctrine marks an advance compared to this, insofar as what takes the place of the element for him represents a higher degree of abstraction than in Empedocles: what Anaxagoras hypostasizes are sensory qualities (*Qualität*) rather than a simple material (*Stoffe*), as is the case in Empedocles. Quite naturally, then, Leucippus represents the third moment of this functionalization of the element, which is equivalent to an ascent in abstraction,[53] since the atom is characterized precisely by the *absence of quality*. The element is "equalized" to the principle (*Grund*),[54] with the epistemological consequence of the distinction between two modes of knowledge, rational (what Democritus will call "genuine") and sensory ("obscure").[55]

Cassirer's brilliant exposition is marked by frequent recourse to teleological formulas, most often hinted at by expressions like "not yet" (*noch nicht*), "already" (*schon*), and "only" (*nur*), but also explicitly asserted sometimes, as for example with regard to the Ionians' contribution to the emergence of the concept of substance: "But it must not be overooked that the *category* of substance in the conceptual determination and terminological fixation that it receives in Aristotle is not yet given here but is only sought—that it forms not so much the starting point of Ionian natural philosophy as rather its goal."[56] Before it is Hegelian, this scheme is clearly already Aristotelian, the *telos* of the mode of thought initiated by the first philosophers being in the present case not the theory of the four causes but the categories constitutive of the principle of reason, with, on the horizon, modern physics as it is incarnated in the names of Kepler, Gassendi, and Helmholz.[57] In this perspective, it is understandable that the decisive turning points that structure Cassirer's account are Pythagoras, the Atomists, and Plato (the great ancient philosophers of scientific knowledge), and that from the beginning Cassirer insisted that the methods of empirical knowledge and experimental science make their appearance at the same time as does the thematization of the guiding concepts of knowledge.[58]

A second feature that is characteristic of Cassirer's narrative is the use he makes of a "reflexive scheme" that associates the concatenation of philosophical positions with a change in perspective, in virtue of which there is a transition from the implicit to the explicit or from the image to the concept. It is to this change of level that his recurrent distinction between "responses" and "form of question" refers or, similarly, between "content of the doctrine" (*Inhalt der Lehre*) and "fundamental form of the approach" (*Grundform der Betrachtung*).[59] This makes it possible to identify in each position considered an imbalance that calls for redress, and this constitutes as it were the motor of historical development.

Indubitably, the combination of these two features—the historical deduction of the categories of scientific thought and the reflexive scheme—brings Cassirer's narrative into the proximity of Hegel.

This is somewhat paradoxical. Certainly, Cassirer always defended Hegel's historiographical project against the criticisms of the positivistic historians, and in particular, with regard to ancient philosophy, against those of his disciple E. Zeller. Thus in the introduction to his *Problem of Knowledge* (and so already in 1906) Cassirer emphasizes that a history conceived along Hegelian lines must be credited with a profound "*idealistic* motive" (Cassirer's emphasis) that remains more relevant than ever, beyond all the "metaphysical aberrations" that it occasions in Hegel himself.[60] What the historian can build upon is not facts, as Zeller wished, but only a hypothesis of knowledge.[61] But, precisely for this reason, Hegel is just as exposed to the objection of having "gone astray" in idealism as Zeller is to that of having yielded to the mirages of historicism. The decisive point is that Hegel set an absolute subject, the spirit, as the foundation and conclusion of history. Despite Cassirer's substitution of the self-discovery of the *logos* for the formula of the self-discovery of the spirit, this criticism bears less upon the reference to the spirit, which Cassirer could easily take over for his own account, than upon the idea of absoluteness. What Hegel can be criticized for is not that he posed a "subject" at the foundation of his narrative, for "every series in a historical development needs a subject":[62] in the present case, this is part of the hypothesis of knowledge. Only, this subject is not an absolute subject. The self-discovery of the *logos* is nothing other than the extrication of thought from determinations that are external to it, the history of a liberation that would have its place within a philosophy of symbolic forms and more generally of culture, insofar as culture is conceived as "the process of the progressive self-liberation of man," which is guided by nothing other than by man himself and his capacities for idealization.[63]

From this point of view, the moment of the birth of philosophy is privileged. More than in later periods, when philosophical reflection has already been constituted and welcomes problems that are imposed upon it from outside, in effect ancient thought creates its own contents, precisely because of the early indistinction between an objective "nature" and a world of the spirit or metaphysics. This is the moment of the "self-determination of philosophy" (*Selbstbestimmung der Philosophie*),[64] which is incarnated in the correlation between thought and being (*Denken/Sein*) in Parmenides, expressing the way in which the discovery of the world and the discovery of thought are entangled with one another (Cassirer speaks of a *Doppelverhältnis*).[65] This is how the concrete character of the first philosophers is explained.[66]

Is Cassirer as different from Hegel as he suggests he is?[67] After all, what matters for Cassirer is showing how the conceptual apparatus of scientific knowledge emerged in the course of an intellectual development marked by advances, with the order in which the systems appeared corresponding at least tendentially to the succession of intellectual determinations. The progress of history coincides with the genesis of an ordered series of concepts. Hence there exists an isomorphism between history and logic in Cassirer no less than in Hegel. It is not because the nature and succession of the intellectual determinations are different from those Hegel proposed that Cassirer escapes from Hegelianism. For, as Cassirer himself has taught us, in the history of philosophy, as in philosophy itself, it is necessary to distinguish between the form of the questions and the particularity of the answers given, and more generally between the form and the contents.

It remains the case that the distinction between form and content and the reflexive scheme that is connected with it are extremely useful for understanding the nature of the Presocratic philosophies and the dynamics of their succession. To say that the *logos* discovers itself is to grant that it is already there. But it is not there as such, in a separate form. On the contrary, what distinguishes it is a certain immanence, which produces at the same time its force and its charm. Reconstructing in his article "*Logos, Dikê, Kosmos*" (1941) the "indissoluble systematic unity" that the ancient Greeks created among the three concepts of Reason, Justice, and the Universe, Cassirer notes "a particular, ever renewed attraction" presented to the historian of philosophy by the exploration of its beginnings, when, in the absence of "the concept of philosophy itself as of its more precise determinations," he must "penetrate into this inner development," or again, "grasp them *in statu nascendi*."[68] The chapter of 1925 explained the status of this gestation more exactly by employing, rightly, the distinction between form and content: "The imperishable value and incomparable attraction of Greek philosophy is grounded not least in the fact that here the *form* of thought grasps the *content* not as something merely external to it, but rather that the form, in the act of configuring the content, in this configuration also first discovers the content."[69] The fact that what is involved here is Greek philosophy in general, and not specifically its beginnings, merely suggests that there exist differences of degree within a history that is globally marked by the inherence of the form within the content. From this point of view, the history of the beginnings is the most interesting one, because the lack of differentiation between form and content, which is destined to become relative, is at its greatest then. As Cassirer writes at the beginning of his exposition, "The first centuries of Greek philosophy can be characterized to a certain extent as the first manifestation of the act of thinking itself: as a thought that in the midst of its pure movement gives to itself its content and its firm configuration."[70]

In general, Cassirer's grand historical narratives (without speaking of the one that he uses at a higher level in the theory of symbolic forms, with the ordered triad of myth, language, and knowledge) are based on an initial imbalance between two moments, the image and the concept, which are always going in the same direction but never manage to coincide.[71] Habermas has given a static interpretation of this imbalance, speaking of the "tension" existing in Cassirer between the thesis of "the equipollence of symbolic worlds that are equally original" and "the trace of a tendency towards liberation that resides in the cultural development" or again, more abstractly, between "expression" (*Ausdruck*) and "meaning" (*Bedeutung*).[72] A tension, as such, calls for a resolution or an overcoming, for which Habermas sees the condition in a systematic relocalization of the language function: instead of assigning it a subordinate function (between myth and knowledge) like Cassirer, it would have been necessary to acknowledge the guiding position that belongs to it both in fact and in Cassirer himself. It remains true that the imbalance is fruitful within the perspective of a philosophical historiography, generally speaking and perhaps even more in the case of the beginnings of philosophy. The fundamental point is that the dynamic that arises from an analysis that refuses the separation of concept and image and instead connects their destiny dialectically is in principle *nonlinear*. If there is indeed progress, it is never only by virtue of the pure concept, not only because the image, from which the concept has come and to which it returns, constitutes an inevitable step, and with that the moment of interpretation, but also because the concept itself, for all its determinations, is in turn nothing more than a new image, itself destined to be overcome. These two levels seem to me to circumscribe the domain of a hermeneutics of properly philosophical texts; taken in conjunction with Weberian "ideas" and "images of the world," the distinction may open the way for a history of the beginnings of Greek philosophy that would be fuller than the one that Cassirer proposes but at the same time would derive inspiration from his perspective. But this would be the object of another study, one that would consider the "Presocratic philosophers" not as a designation, but for themselves.

- oh no oh no   Nietzche says pts
                                        deception
Hegel - Teleogical ←
   • spirit manifesting itself
   • end contained in the beginning

50   50
x20   20
———   ——
00   00
  0   1,000
1200

Nietzches - no purpose
        in history
     - no rational
        trajectory

Laks - Directionallity
       w/o full teleology
future is open, not
    already determined

NOTES

1. Eberhard (1788) 1796, 47. The reference is provided by Paquet, in Paquet and Lafrance 1995, 26.
2. Plato, *Phaedo* 96a; emphasis added. Cf. SOCR. D7 LM.
3. "For all of the writings of the ancients are entitled *On Nature*: those of Melissus, Parmenides, Empedocles, Alcmaeon as well as of Gorgias, Prodicus, and all the others." Galen, *On the Elements according to Hippocrates* 1.9 (p. 134, 16–19/De Lacy = 24A2DK, ALCM. D2 LM). On the history of this title, see Schmalzriedt 1970.
4. See below, chap. 3, pp. 45–47.
5. For the date of this treatise, which has been the object of scholarly debate (cf. Schiefsky 2005, 63–64), see the conclusions of Jouanna 1990, 85. The reference to Empedocles not only provides a terminus *post quem*, it also suggests a certain topicality.
6. On the meaning of the term "sophist," see below, chap. 3, pp. 47–48; on the comparison between philosophy and pictorial art, see ibid., p. 46.
7. Cf. 31A71DK, MED. 7b; and EMP. 56 LM.
8. Fr. 910 (59A30DK, DRAM. T43aLM). Plato alludes to this debate during the confrontation between Socrates and Callicles in his *Gorgias* (484e, 485e, 489e). On the provenance of the fragment, see Kambitsis 1972, 130. The play is generally dated to the 410s (Kambitsis 1972, XXXIs). On metrical grounds, Jouan and Van Looy (2002, 220–21) defend a somewhat older date, between 437 and 419.
9. *Dissoi Logoi* (90DK = DISS. LM) §8.1. I adhere to the traditional dating of this text. Burnyeat (1998), who thinks that it is a Pyrrhonian exercise, suggests a later date, in the second half of the fourth century BCE.
10. There is no good English equivalent for *hoi phusikoi*; I have preferred "naturalists" to "physicians" or "physicists" as being slightly less misleading. In any case, one cannot avoid "physics" for the domain that is studied by *hoi phusikoi*.
11. Xenophon, *Memorabilia* 1.1.11; emphasis added. The "world" (*kosmos*) also appears here as a technical expression, as is indicated by the phrase *ho kaloumenos kosmos*, as the type of study that takes it for its object.

12. Plato, *Lysis* 214a–b (though the expression might be a hendiadys).

13. Plato, Philebus 59a. But the more detailed expression is found in *Timaeus* 47a: *hê peri tês tou pantos phuseôs zêtêsis.*

14. The references can be found in Bonitz's *Index Aristotelicus* (*hoi peri phuseôs*, 838b26ff.; *phusiologoi*, 835b40ff.; *hoi phusikoi*, 835b3ff.).

15. See the title of Kahn's (1960) 1994 classical study: *Anaximander and the Origins of Greek Cosmology.* There is every reason to suppose that Thales's project did not present this systematic character.

16. Naddaf maintains that the narrative of the development of human civilization was part of the genre from the beginning (see, e.g., 2005, 28–29, 112); I see no decisive evidence for this; it was, rather, an optional development that the paradigm naturally authorized.

17. Plato, *Protagoras* 315c5–6.

18. Hippocrates, *Fleshes* 1.2.

19. Plato, *Phaedo* 96b1–c1 (cf. SOCR. D7 LM).

20. I adopt here the chronology defended by Mansfeld 1979, 55–57; and 1980, 87–88.

21. Fr. 913 Kannicht (59A20 DK = DRAM. T43bLM); emphasis added.

22. Our sole source of information on this issue is Diogenes Laertius, *Lives of Eminent Philosophers* 9.57; but this text can also be read in such a way as to mean that the philosopher concerned is Anaxagoras and not Diogenes (see Laks 2008a, 111–12). For a recent defense of this interpretation, see Fazzo 2009, 162 with n6.

23. Plato, *Apology of Socrates* 18a–b, 19a–c. On Socrates and the Presocratic philosophers in Aristophanes's *Clouds*, see Laks and Saetta-Cottone 2013.

24. Aristophanes, *Clouds* 225–36. It was Diels ([1881] 1969) who first showed that the Socrates of the *Clouds* speaks the language of Diogenes. See also Vander Waerdt 1994, 61. For a criticism of this reading and a preference for Archelaus, whose presence in Athens cannot be doubted, as that of Diogenes can be (cf. above, chap. 1, n. 22), see Fazzo 2009; and Betegh 2013, 94–95.

25. Plato later supplied an impressive theoretical justification for this amalgam, obviously detached from Socrates, within the framework of his celebrated refutation of atheism in the tenth book of the *Laws* (889b1–890a10).

26. Plato, *Apology* 19c. Cf. Aristophanes, *Clouds* 180–95.

27. 1.1.11. (cf. SOCR. D3 LM).

28. Diogenes Laertius, *Lives of Eminent Philosophers* 1.18; 2.16; 2.20–21.

29. Cf. Plato, *Phaedo*, 96a6–9. Cf. above, chap. 1, p. 6 n. 2.

30. Diogenes Laertius, *Lives of Eminent Philosophers* 2.16. Vander Waerdt (1994, 61), relying on Aristophanes, suggests that Socrates had once been a follower of Diogenes of Apollonia.

31. A celebrated example is the meeting he arranges between an old Parmenides and a young Socrates in the *Parmenides*.

32. Cicero, *Tusculan Disputations* 5.5.

33. Cicero, *Tusculan Disputations* 5.6.

34. The first attested list appears in Plato's *Protagoras* 343a. It comprises the names of Thales of Miletus, Pittacus of Mytilene, Bias of Priene, Solon of Athens ("our Solon"), Cleobulus of Lindos, Myson of Chenae, and Chilon of Sparta. On the history of the list, see Buisine 2002.

35. Cicero, *Tusculan Disputations* 5.9; cf. Diogenes Laertius, *Lives of Eminent Philosophers* 1.12 (= Heraclides of Pontus Fr. 87 Wehrli =84 Schütrumpf; cf. PYTHS. R29 LM). Cicero is *not* referring here to the Platonic distinction between "wisdom" that would be the privilege of the gods and an "aspiration to wisdom" (or philosophy) belonging to men alone.

36. Xenophon, *Memorabilia* 1.1.14. This question already figures in Plato's *Sophist* 242c5 ("how many beings are there and in what number?"); cf. Isocrates, *Antidosis* 268. Mansfeld (1986, sect. 4 and 5) has insisted on the importance of these pre-Aristotelian lists for the history of ancient doxography.

37. Xenophon, *Memorabilia* 1.1.13–14 (DOX. T5 LM); emphasis added.

38. Aristotle, *Metaphysics* 1.3 983b8–10. Aristotle uses in turn "substance" (*ousia*) in b10, "principle" in b11, "nature" in b13, and "substrate" in b16. Cf. 984a30–32.

39. The double meaning of the term *phusis*, which can refer both to the natural growth of a thing and to its intrinsic nature, is already present in its first (and sole) occurrence in Homer, at *Odyssey* 10.303.

40. See above, chap. 1, n. 3.

41. *Against the Physicists* 2.46.

42. I follow here the terminology adopted by Elkana 1986.

43. If there is no wind, the oars will be used (according to the interpretation of the metaphor that Menander gives, Fr 183 Kassel-Austin). If the final end is out of reach, the philosopher will content himself with the form.

44. *Phaedo* 95a–e.

45. *Phaedo* 96a.

46. *Timaeus* 46c–d.

47. *Phaedo* 97c.

48. *Phaedo* 98c.

49. *Phaedo* 99d1.

50. *Phaedo* 98e.

51. On the Platonization of Socrates in the autobiographical narrative of the *Phaedo*, see Babut 1978.

52. The possible relation of the formal cause to the final causality, of which the requirement had been formulated in the criticism of Anaxagoras, is not thematized within the *Phaedo*. This is, of course, not by chance: this question is one of the cruxes of Platonism. It should be remarked that, together with the concept of contrariety, the two causalities, formal and final, will be at the center of Aristotle's *Physics*.

53. *Meteorologica* 2.2, 355b32–34.

54. The expression, in *Metaphysics* 983b6–7, is applied to the new way of philosophizing introduced by Thales (cf. 983b20). It is understood in relation to Plato, of whom Aristotle says later that his teaching is located "after the philosophers about whom we have spoken" (987a29). The first occurrence, in 982b11, is applied to a philosophy that is even earlier, contemporary with mankind's first experiences of astonishment.

55. The fact that the name of "Socrates" serves to illustrate the concept of a substantial "nature" (*phusis*), which "most of the first philosophers" glimpse when they pose one and the same material principle subsisting beyond generations and corruptions (*Metaphysics* 983b12–16), could indeed be read as the symbol of this continuity.

56. *Metaphysics* 987b1–2.

57. *Metaphysics* 987b2–4

58. *Metaphysics* 13.4, 1078b17–31. On the distinction between what concerns Socrates and what concerns Democritus in this passage, see Narcy 1997.

59. *Parts of Animals* 1.2 642a24–31.

60. *Parts of Animals* 1.2 642a17.

61. Diogenes Laertius, *Lives of Eminent Philosophers* 1.13–15. To the degree that what is involved is the history of post-Socratic philosophy, one might well question the appropriateness of this bipartition, of which the first branch, in Diogenes Laertius, ends, after a double ramification at the level of Socrates, and then of Plato, with an Academician (Clitomachus), a Stoic (Chrysippus), and a Peripatetic (Theophrastus), while the second continues in a direct line down to Epicurus. But a certain legitimacy may be granted to it, as far as the beginnings go, if one discerns in the opposition between East and West two distinct intellectual orientations (without being able to derive an authorization for

doing so from Diogenes Laertius, who remains with a purely geographical distribution). While the Milesians' reflection, in Ionia, has for its first privileged frame of reference explanations of a cosmological order, Magna Graecia is strongly marked by eschatological concerns, without excluding these cosmological considerations.

62. Diogenes Laertius *Lives of Eminent Philosophers* 1.14.

63. See chap. 1, pp. 8–9.

64. *Lives of Eminent Philosophers* 1.18, which adds, "And, starting with Zeno of Elea, the dialectical part." In this case, the principle of correspondence between divisions of philosophy and periods of its history is no longer valid. The statement reads like an implicit correction: Socrates is not the inventor of dialectic, but instead, before him, it was Zeno.

65. *Lives of Eminent Philosophers* 2.16 and 20–21.

66. See above, chap. 1, p. 1.

Chapter 2: Presocratics: The Modern Constellation

1. This collection, in the version revised by W. Kranz, remains the edition of reference to this very day (Diels-Kranz 1951–1952).

2. Aristotle, *Metaphysics* 1.3. 986b6–7.

3. Cf. Krug 1815. S. Karsten, one of the greatest experts on the Presocratic philosophers of the first half of the nineteenth century, thought of entitling the collection he planned *The Remains of the Works of the Ancient Greek Philosophers, Especially of Those Who Flourished before Plato* (*Philosophorum graecorum veterum praesertim qui ante Platonem floruerunt operum reliquiae*). Only three parts were published, Xenophanes (1830), Parmenides (1835), and Empedocles (1838).

4. Cf. Schleiermacher (1815).

5. Cf. above, chap. 1, p. 10.

6. On the use of Cicero's formula by popular philosophy, see Ernesti, "*De philosophia populari*," (1754) in Beck and Thouard 1995, 372.

7. Schleiermacher (1815) 1835, 293.

8. Schleiermacher (1815) 1835, 289, from which these quotations derive.

9. Hegel 1995, 102 and 352.

10. Zeller (1844/1852) 1919/1923. Zeller was very interested in the problem of periodization in history in general. See in particular the section entitled "Die Hauptentwicklungen der griechischen Philosophie" ("The Principal Developments of Greek Philosophy"), I/1, 210–227 (210–218 for the period that interests us here).

11. Zeller (1844/1852) 1919/1923, 217.

12. Diels's collection could not fail to impose itself against Mullach's mediocre one, published in 1860, of which moreover the full title reveals the problems that could be created by the fluctuation in periodization before Zeller: *Fragmenta philosophorum graecorum, I: Poeseos philosophicae caeterorumque ante Socratem philosophorum quae supersunt, II. Pythagoreos, Sophistas, Cynicos et Chalcidii in Priorem Timaei platonici partem commentarios continens*, Paris 1860/1867. It is not only the Sophists, but also the Pythagoreans and the Cynics who are separated from the "Presocratics." The Sophists are not included in Mansfeld and Primavesi's 2011 collection, nor are they currently part of the project *Traditio Praesocratica* published by De Gruyter.

13. See Borsche 1985 and Most 1995.

14. Cf. Nietzsche 1995 and 2006. The title appears for the first time in the program of his courses for the winter semester 1869–1870. Nietzsche delivers the course later in 1872 (summer semester) and in 1875–1876 (winter and summer semesters). On the chronology of Nietzsche's teaching, see Janz 1974.

15. See Nietzsche's *Philosophy in the Tragic Age of the Greeks* (*Die Philosophie im tragischen Zeitalter der Griechen*) in Nietzsche (1980) 1:799–872, §2.

16. See §261 of Nietzsche (1980) 2:214–218, *Human All Too Human*, partial quotations *supra*, chap. 2, pp. 26 and 30. Nietzsche's evolution can be studied in the fragments of 1870/1875 (Nietzsche 1980, vols. 7 and 8).

17. Schopenauer (1850) 1974, 36–37.

18. Schopenhauer (1850) 1974, 35.

19. These excursuses have been studied by Anders in Schlechta and Anders 1962.

20. It was by the mediation of W. Capelle (who in 1935 had published a collection devoted to the Presocratics) that Freud adopted the use of the term *Trieb* to refer to Love and Hate in Empedocles. Freud saw his "dualistic theory according to which an instinct of death or of destruction or aggression claims equal rights as a partner of Eros as manifested in the libido," a theory that had encountered only a weak resonance, corroborated by "one of the great thinkers of ancient Greece" (Freud [1937] 1964, 245–247); cf. Bollack (1985) 2016.

21. Nietzsche 2006, 27, 60, 118, and 126.

22. See the two prefaces to *Philosophy in the Tragic Age of the Greeks*. In his *Geschichte der Renaissance in Italien* (*The Civilization of the Renaissance*

in Italy) (1860), J. Burckhardt devotes a section to the "Development of the Individual." His *Griechische Kulturgeschichte* delivered in courses starting in 1880, grants a central role to the category of "free personality," but hardly ever mentions the Presocratics (Burckhardt [1898/ 1902] 1977, 3:339–378; cf. Laks 2006).

23. Cf. Nietzsche (1873) 1980.

24. Nietzsche 1980, 6:446 (*R. Wagner at Bayreuth*, §4). Nietzsche says not "Parmenides" but "the Eleatics."

25. Cf. next note.

26. Hölderlin 1969, 941.

27. Nietzsche 1980, 8:6 [13].

28. Nietzsche 1980, 8:6 [12].

29. See also *Twilight of the Idols*, "The Problem of Socrates," in which Socrates is described as a tyrant over his own passions. Nietzsche 1980, 6:67–73.

30. Nietzsche 1980, 8:6 [11]. The same structure as what Heidegger will call *phusis* or *alêtheia* can be recognized here.

31. See Nietzsche 1980, 1:801.

32. See Nietzsche 1980, 6:312–313 (*Ecce Homo: Die Geburt der Tragödie*, 3).

33. I do not discuss in this essay the specific uses Heidegger made of the Presocratics. What he has to say about the "originary thinkers" (cf., e.g., Heidegger 1982, 2) derives from a philosophical mythology for which the analysis would require other instruments than those that can be applied here. However, some general features of his approach are taken up by Gadamer, whose position is considered below, chap. 6, pp. 80–84.

34. Kranz in Diels-Kranz 1951–1952, viii.

35. Schmalzriedt 1970, 83n1.

36. On the use Blumenberg makes of this notion, see below, chap. 5, pp. 75–76.

37. This distinction lies at the basis of the classic study by Burkert 1972.

38. On the Derveni papyrus in general, see Betegh 2004. For a synthesis concerning the cultural and religious context of fourth-century Macedonia, see Piano 2016, 349–356.

39. See above, chap. 1, n. 54.

40. Nietzsche 1980, 2:217.

41. Socrates does not play any decisive role in Heidegger. In any case, the expression "originary thinkers" is just as exposed to erroneous representations as are other ones, as Heidegger emphasizes: "The originary easily passes for being imperfect, unfinished, coarse. It is also called 'the primitive.' This is how the opinion comes about according to which

the thinkers who precede Plato and Aristotle are 'primitive thinkers' "
(Heidegger 1982, 2).

42. Cassirer 1925 (this was already one of the criteria mentioned by Eberhard [1788] 1796). Windelband (1891) distinguishes a cosmological
period (*kosmologische Periode*) from an anthropological period (*anthro-
pologische Periode*).

43. Oppermann 1929, esp. 30–31. Nestle had already used the term in his
supplements to Zeller (1844/52) 1919/1923, 1:225n: "Presocratic or
more precisely pre-Sophistic philosophy."

44. On the concept of the "Archaic age," see Heuss 1946 and Most 1989. In
the history of philosophy, the term "archaic" is used, for example, by
Hoffmann 1947. See already Reinhardt (1916) 1977, 52.

45. Mansfeld and Primavesi 2011, 9–10.

46. Long 1999, 5–10; cf. 21n33.

47. Cf. the title of the classic book of Burnet 1892: *Early Greek Philosophy*.
By the same token, Glenn W. Most and I have entitled our collection of
texts published in the Loeb Library (2016) *Early Greek Philosophy*. It
includes a chapter on Socrates.

48. Baur 1876; cf. Fascher 1959.

49. "In his *On Nature*, which is the only one of his writings that has reached
me" (Simplicius, *Commentary on Aristotle's Physics*, p. 151, 28–29 Diels.
Scholars disagree about which library Simplicius used. I. Hadot (1987,
esp. 19) maintained that it was not the Academy at Athens, but the library of Haran, during his exile in Persia.

50. On the presence of Empedocles in the Byzantine age, see Primavesi
2002, 197–201. On the manuscript of Aurispa, see Mansfeld 1994.

51. See above, chap. 2, p. 29.

52. Martin and Primavesi 1999.

CHAPTER 3: PHILOSOPHY

1. *Sophist* 242c (cf. above, chap. 1, n. 36).

2. See above, chap. 1, p. 15.

3. In very different genres, Reinhardt (1916) 1977 and Cherniss (1935)
1964 are representative here. For Nietzsche's position, cf. above, chap. 1,
pp. 11–12.

4. See in this sense, e.g., Havelock 1996.

5. For the category of "sages" (now widespread), see Nightingale 2004, 29–
30; for the distinction between science and philosophy, see Mansfeld
1985; for the shamanic model, see Kingsley 1995, (1999) 2001, 2003.

6. See especially Gigon 1945; Diller (1946) 1966; Fränkel 1975, 108n30.

7. See the collection of essays entitled *From Myth to Reason?* (Buxton 1999), which takes off from the work that has become the symbol of the contested thesis, W. Nestle's *Vom Mythos zum Logos*. In the introduction to that book, published in 1940, one reads that "to travel along the path that goes from myth to reason, to rise up from spiritual immaturity to maturity, is a privilege that seems to have remained reserved for the Aryan peoples as the race that is best endowed by nature. And among these, this development cannot be traced anywhere else more clearly than among the Greeks" (6). This declaration does not really affect the content of the book.

8. See the analysis of Vernant's thesis on the rise of Greek rationality, "daughter of the city" below, chap. 4, p. 57.

9. It is significant from this point of view that Vernant, who systematically criticized the notion of the "Greek miracle" (see *supra*, chap. 4, p. 55), gave the title "From Myth to Reason" to the final section of the collection *Myth and Thought among the Greeks* (Vernant [1965] 2006).

10. The phrase is Buxton's, from Buxton 1999, 4.

11. See Cassirer 1946.

12. Spencer (1862) 1908, 291 (§125).

13. For a concise and stimulating presentation of the data, see Calame 1991.

14. It is a "detailed, authoritative speech act" (Martin 1989, 13n42; cf. 68). The minimalist meaning "rumor," which M. Detienne felt obliged hyperbolically to set in opposition to the totality of the meanings derived from "the invention of mythology" (both Ancient and Modern; see Detienne 1986), is only one of the possibilities within a complex semantic field.

15. Burkert (1979, 32) distinguishes mythical "sequence" from rational "consequence."

16. Cf. Calame 1991, 187.

17. *Sophist* 242c8, 244a3–b4.

18. The term "nature" does not refer here to the world of natural phenomena, but to what, in a given thing, persists under its possible modifications, i.e., to the nature of things and not to natural things. This does not in the least prevent the "philosophers of nature" from practicing natural philosophy, but from Aristotle's point of view this is just as contingent as the fact that for Socrates ethics was the privileged domain of investigation for questions touching upon definition (see above, chap. 1, p. 16).

19. *Letter to Pythocles* §§104, 115, 116.
20. See above, chap. 1, pp. 12–13.
21. Cf. above, chap. 3, n. 5
22. Cf. Zhmud 2006, 18–20. For the classification of Anaximenes and Anaximander under the rubric of men of science, see *supra*, chap. 3, p. 35.
23. These arguments have been developed by G. E. R. Lloyd more than once; see, e.g., Lloyd 2002.
24. *Birds* 992–1020.
25. Lloyd 2002, 48–49.
26. Ibid., 44–45.
27. Ibid., 53 (Lloyd's translation of the French original).
28. Nightingale 1995, 14; cf. Nightingale 2004, 30.
29. On the particular plasticity of philosophy, see below, chap. 3, pp. 48–49.
30. See above, chap. 1, pp. 2–4.
31. Cf. Burkert 1970.
32. See above, chap. 1, p. 10.
33. For an attempt to give credence to Cicero's report, see Riedweg 2002, 120–128. The classic discussion is found in Burkert 1960. See also Gottschalk 1980, 29–33.
34. For the problem posed by the interpretation of this fragment, see below, pp. 44–45.
35. *Republic* 5.475d.
36. Moreover, this is a meaning that the term was never to lose and that was used, starting with Isocrates, by the advocates of general culture against philosophy itself, whose new contours Plato had recently established firmly.
37. Thucydides, *History of the Peloponesian War* 2.40, with the commentary of Frede 2004, 21–22.
38. Herodotus, *The Histories* 1.30. In this sentence, the conjunction of the terms *philosophein* and *theôria*, both of them taken in a prephilosophical sense (*theôria* in the sense of the observation of mores and customs), is evidently noteworthy.
39. Cf. Text ad n. 34 above.
40. 21B35 DK = HER. D40 LM.
41. 21B40 DK = HER. D20 LM.
42. For my part, I incline to the second interpretation, which seems to me more interesting and also more plausible.
43. See Wiese 1963, 258–259f. Cf. also Burkert 1960, 171. Scholars who attribute to Pythagoras the invention of the word "philosophy" argue

from its presence in Heraclitus, who cites the name of Pythagoras (but pejoratively) in Fr. 21 B129 DK = HER. D26 LM.

44. See above, chap. 1, pp. 2–3.

45. Jouanna 1990, 208n8; Vegetti 1998. Schiefsky (2005, 309–310) prefers "art of writing": the Hippocratic writer would be attacking the authors of literary compositions, who are no more than that.

46. 31 B23 DK = EMP. D60 LM.

47. Herodotus, *On Ancient Medicine*, chap. 1.1–3; 13; 15–16.

48. Cf. Pohlenz 1918, who suggests that the rapprochement is founded on the idea that painting, like philosophy, belongs to a category of art that was considered secondary and not necessary (cf. the position reported by Plato, *Laws* 10.889d3).

49. 31B111 DK = EMP. D43 LM. On Empedocles as a thaumaturge, see Vegetti 1996.

50. See chap. 1, pp. 5–6.

51. Thus it is logical that the meteorologists are not presented as attacking one another, but as shaping the opinion of their public in one direction and another, a distinction that could naturally be contested. Parmenides's goddess recurs explicitly to athletic terminology to say that no mortal will ever surpass her adressee with regard to cosmology (28B8.60 DK = PARM. D8.66 LM).

52. On the meaning of the term, see Kerferd (1981)1999, chap. 3.

53. Fr. 3 Laks.

54. *Euthydemus* 305c6 (84 B6 DK = PROD. D7 LM).

55. See Cassirer (1935) 1979. Plato's great rival Isocrates presents an interesting case, since his conception of philosophy as practical knowledge, indissociable from rhetoric, did not impose itself as philosophically legitimate in the end, even if it continued to be considered so for a long time during Antiquity.

56. Hesiod, *Works and Days* 17–26.

57. "... if some difference manifests itself between the views we have stated and those of the men who study these things, we must appreciate both, but follow the more accurate ones." *Metaphysics* 12.8 1073b14–17.

58. *History of Animals* 511b31–513b11. Diogenes, who does not distinguish betwen veins and arteries, speaks of *phlebes*, translated as "vessels" (see Laks [1983] 2008a, 98).

59. Simplicius, *Commentary on Aristotle's Physics* p. 153.15–16. Diels.

60. Cf. Laks (1983) 2008a, 98–99 on Fr. 10 Laks (64B6 DK = DIOG. D27 LM). On the question of the number of Diogenes's books, see ibid. 46–48.

61. Cf. Theophrastus, *On Sensation* §§43, 44, 45.
62. For sensation, cf. T8 Laks (64A19 DK = DIOG. D34, 35, 36, 38, 39, 41, 42 LM); reproduction, T15 Laks (A24 DK = D28a LM); digestion, cf. Theophrastus, *On Sensation* §44; and Laks (1983) 2008a, 175.
63. Zhmud 2006, 18–19. On the complexities of demarcating ancient science from philosophy, see also the second section in Zhmud and Kouprianov, forthcoming.
64. Popper (1958–1959) 1965.
65. See the debate in Lloyd (1972) 1991.
66. So Mansfeld 1985, 56.
67. Aristotle, *Metaphysics* 1.3 983b13. The fact that what is involved is an interpretation by Aristotle rather than a thesis maintained by Thales (see Laks 2004a; 2007), is not relevant here.
68. See above, chap. 1, pp. 4–6.

CHAPTER 4: RATIONALITY

1. On this theme in general see Momigliano 1975.
2. Hippias 86B6 DK = HIPPIAS D22 LM; cf. Plato (or pseudo-Plato), *Epinomis* 987d; Aristotle, *On Philosophy*, Fr. 6 Ross (= Diogenes Laertius, *Life of Eminent Philosophers* 1.6). The meaning of this thesis is changed if one combines it with a cyclic conception of history, found in various passages in Aristotle, according to which civilization is periodically destroyed by cataclysms (*Metaphysics* 12.8 1074b1–14; cf. *On the Heavens* 1.3 270b13–20; *Meteorologica* 1.3 339b27–30; *Politics* 8.10 1329b25–29; and *On Philosophy*, Fr. 8 Ross): the Greeks, who bring to perfection what exists among the barbarians only potentially, also precede them, inasmuch as actuality precedes potentiality. On the usage made of the idea of the barbarian origin of philosophy in Renaissance syncretism and Marsilio Ficino, cf. below, chap. 5, n. 26.
3. In fact, Diogenes Laertius's position is perhaps more complex than is suggested by the tone he adopts; cf. Laks 2015.
4. The cities of southern Italy (Magna Graecia), where first Pythagorean philosophy develops, then Eleatic, are colonies in which the culture of their mother cities is transmitted. On the history of Miletus, see Gorman 2001.
5. The work of Walter Burkert is fundamental here. Burkert 2004 provides a clear and balanced synthesis on this subject.
6. Burkert 2004, 68–69.

7. Burkert 2004, 69. For the general problematic of the relationship between the first Greek cosmologies and Near Eastern models, see also Hölscher 1968, chap. 1.

8. Burkert 2004, 66; cf. Burkert (1994–1995) 2003, 194.

9. Burkert 2004, 67; cf. Kingsley 1992.

10. Burkert 2004, 66–67, on the basis of Livingstone 1986. I must say that my own consultation of Livingstone's book did not convince me that the "explanatory work" reflected in the documents he edits is truly comparable to the cosmological approach of the Milesians, even if Livingstone, commenting on "a type of speculation ... concerned with equating groups of closely related parts or aspects of the natural world with groups of deities," writes that "the ancient [scil. Babylonian] philosophers endeavoured to find ways of making existing theology accord more precisely with the facts of the natural world" (71).

11. Burkert 2004, 4. On the relatively late appearance of the term "philosophy" as a technical term, see above, chap. 3, p. 45.

12. Burkert 2004, 68; cf. Burkert 1992, 308–310. Burkert cites in this connection, evidently for the use of the term *logos*, a fragment of Eudemus (a student of Aristotle), who speaks with regard to Anaximander of the "*logos* about sizes and distances" (Fr. 146 Wehrli).

13. Burkert 2004, 14 (cf. 69). On the same page, Burkert notes, "No doubt the Greek success had to do with freedom of enterprise, of speech, of imagination, even of religion."

14. This is why Popper ([1958–1959] 1965) was able to find among the Presocratics the very same principle of a critical rationalism to which he advocated a return.

15. Vernant (1962) 1982.

16. Cf. below, n. 17.

17. Renan (1878)1948, 397.

18. Renan 1883, chap. 2.

19. See Vernant (1957) 2006, 371.

20. Cf. Meyerson (1948) 1987.

21. Meier (1980) 1990, 29.

22. Cornford 1912 and 1952.

23. Vernant (1957) 2006, 371 ("mental mutation").

24. Vernant (1957) 2006, 397. This conclusion is repeated unchanged in Vernant (1962) 1982, 132.

25. Gernet (1945 and 1956) 1968; (1945) 1983. On Gernet's work and his development, see Humphreys 1978, 84–85; as well as Donato 1983.

26. On the bipartition of the history of philosophy in Diogenes Laertius, see above, chap. 1, p. 17.

27. Probably impelled by a desire for symmetry, Vernant (1957) 2006, 388 moves rather quickly over this affirmation, which does not seem to me to be justified.

28. According to Vernant, this separation does not imply that the Ionian thinkers are cut off from the social dimension; on the contrary, it is the condition of possibility for attributing to them the function of legislators; cf. Vernant (1957) 2006, 388.

29. Vernant (1957) 2006, 386–387.

30. Vernant (1957) 2006, 389, 390, 396.

31. This thesis has been taken up by Seaford (2004, 188–209) against Vernant's political model.

32. Vernant (1957) 2006, 392–396. See the notion of the "autonomous path" in Meyerson (1948) 1987.

33. The image of the "focus" was introduced by Owen (1986, 184) in order to give an account of the relation between a series of terms that are semantically irreducible to one another but that all refer to a single term (*pros hen*).

34. The question is raised by M. Caveing in Vernant (1975) 1996, 113.

35. Meier 1986, 69.

36. Vernant mentions the name of Weber one time, but not in a significant way, in his review (1956) of the French translation by F. Bourricaud of a selection of texts by T. Parsons published in 1955 by Plon under the title *Eléments pour une sociologie de l'action* [*Elements for a Sociology of Action*] (in Vernant 1995, 2:627). The index of Gernet 1983 includes only one reference to Max Weber, not for the text of Gernet himself but for a phrase by the editor R. di Donato, speaking, with regard to a critical review by Gernet ("How to Characterize the Economy of Ancient Greece," 1933) of an "unconscious but significant encounter between the school of Max Weber and French sociology" (Donato 1983, 410).

37. Cambiano 1988, ix.

38. Vernant (1962) 1982, 132. It is certainly not by chance that Vernant, together with M. Detienne, became interested later in "cunning intelligence," which is repressed by objectivizing rationality (Detienne and Vernant [1974] 1991).

39. There is a certain tension between this interpretation and the idea that secularization bears not less upon the social than upon the theological; see above, chap. 4, n. 28. For criticism of the egalitarian interpretation

that Vernant gives of Anaximander's cosmology, see Sassi 2007 and Laks 2008b.

40. See below, pp. 62–63.

41. See the pertinent critique by Seaford 2004, 175–189.

42. The criterion of Panhellenicity casts an interesting light on the question of the emergence of rationality, since it is manifestly already at work in the treatment of the traditional myths in Homer and after him (see Nagy 1979, 7–9). Moreover, the conditions of the concrete operation of this Panhellenic rationality, as far as Greek philosophy is concerned, have sometimes seemed problematic: the rhythm with which philosophy develops on the territory of Greece presupposes a rapid circulation of intellectual information, but it is not easy to imagine the networks involved; nonetheless they must be presupposed.

43. Burckhardt (1898/1902) 1977, 4:84–117.

44. For the argument relative to truth claims, cf. Humphreys 1996, 6. For the question of the relation between writing and the emergence of philosophy, see Laks 2001, 2007.

45. This point is emphasized by Schluchter 1988.

46. Weber 2016, 101–105. Capitalism is not only the last term of the series; it is also its reason, insofar as in Weber's eyes it constitutes "the power that weighs most heavily on the destiny of our modern life" (105).

47. Weber 2016, 280.

48. Weber 1989, 83.

49. On the "egotism" that marks the beginnings of Greek philosophy, see Lloyd 1997, and previously Burckhardt, (1898/1902) 1977, 3:346. For the relation between philosophers and politics, cf. Burckhardt, (1898/1902) 1977, 3:344.

50. Weber 1989, 480.

51. See Schluchter 1979 as well as Habermas (1981) 1987, vol. 1, chap. 2 ("Weber's Theory of Rationalization"), 168–178.

52. Cf. above, chap. 1, n. 61.

53. Weber 1989, 101. By "ideal interest" Weber seems to be referring to values, like for example honor, or else to salvation. The extension of the Ideas is evidently larger.

CHAPTER 5: ORIGINS

1. The term is taken up and discussed by Weil 1975. For the use historians have made of it, see Schwartz 1975 and Humphreys (1986) 2004.

2. See above, chap. 4, p. 56.

3. There is never a breakthrough except for us, says Weil, commenting on Jaspers (Weil 1975, 21–22 and 36).

4. Jaspers (1949) 1953, chap. 1, 1–21; Weil 1975, 21.

5. For the chronological considerations, see Burkert 1994–1995, 184–185. For the fundamental criticism, see Assmann 1989. Jaspers refers to China, India, Iran, Jews and Greeks; cf. Jaspers (1949) 1953, 51.

6. Burckhardt 2000, 134.

7. I return to this question in chap. 6.

8. Evidently the large "we" of humanity must be distinguished from the more specific "we" of a given civilization, in the present case, our own. The Greek breakthrough and the Jewish breakthrough are distinguished from the Chinese breakthrough by the kinds of historical relation that links us with them.

9. Vernant (1962) 1982, chap. 7. Cf. already Aristotle, *Metaphysics* 14.4 1091a33–91b7.

10. *Theogony*, 454–500, with West's commentary on lines 454 and 497. See also line 48, athetized by West because the Muses there are said to sing Zeus "in first and last place," whereas they have just stated that they sing him "in second place," after the descendants of Gaia and Ouranus (on this point, see Vernant [1962] 1982, chap. 7; and Betegh 2004, 173; cf. 219–220).

11. Pherecydes 7 B1 DK = D5 LM; cf. Aristotle, *Metaphysics* 14.4 1091b8–10.

12. See Simplicius, *Commentary on Aristotle's Physics*, p. 24.15f. Diels (= Theophrastus, *Opinions of the Philosophers*, Fr. 2 Diels). According to a different interpretation, Anaximander would have been the first to call his principle "unlimited."

13. For the use Cassirer, for example, makes of the distinction between "origin" and "beginning" among the Presocratics, see below, chap. 6, p. 87.

14. Saïd 1975, 6.

15. Bernal 1987–1991. For a critical reaction, see Lefkowitz 1996.

16. In a period in which the world had become considerably enlarged and the Greek heritage was confronted more directly with other ones, Clement redirects and amplifies themes that go back already to Plato and Aristotle. On the relation, hypothetical but very illuminating, between Clement and Diogenes, see Canfora 1992 and Ramelli 2004. On the character of Diogenes Laertius's prologue, which is probably more ambiguous than is often suspected, see Laks 2015.

17. Idel 2001, 320.

18. Idel 2001, 329. The quotation appears in Scholem 1969, 98.

19. Idel (2001, 315) quotes Bloom 1987, 69.

20. Renan 1863, 8.

21. What Zarader (1986) calls the "originary words" (see also Courtine 1999).

22. The texts have been collected by Kleingünther 1933; see also Thraede 1962.

23. See Laks 2004a.

24. Simplicius, *Commentary on Aristotle's Physics*, 23, 29–32 Diels = Theophrastus, *Opinions of the Philosophers*, Fr. 1 Diels.

25. See above, chap. 1, pp. 5–10.

26. One would also have to take into account the specific stakes that are connected in the perspective of Neoplatonism and of Renaissance syncretism with the question of the origin of philosophy as being "barbarian," i.e., non-Greek, and especially Egyptian. This is the conception with which the historiography of the Enlightenment (represented especially by J. Brucker) breaks by imposing Thales (cf. Blackwell 1997), as it were playing off the Aristotle of the *Metaphysics* against the Aristotle of his *On Philosophy* (cf. above, chap. 3, p. 53 and n. 2).

27. See chap. 1, pp. 5, 10.

28. This is the meaning of the great debate on the number and birthdates of the various "Renaissances" (cf. Panofsky 1960, chap. 1).

29. Blumenberg (1966) 1983, 462.

30. Salamis gave rise to a famous synchronism, doubled by a spatial component: in 480, Aeschylus fought against the Medes, Sophocles danced to celebrate the victory, and Euripides was born on the island (cf. Tyrell 2012, 20).

31. Blumenberg (1966) 1983, 460.

32. Chapter 16 of Musil's *The Man without Qualities* (1995) provides a striking description of a situation of this type.

33. Cassirer (1922) 1969, 54.

34. Cassirer (1922) 1969, 55–56.

35. See chap. 1, pp. 17–18.

36. See the works of G. E. R. Lloyd, in particular Lloyd 1997.

37. Saïd 1975, 34.

38. 21B18 DK = D53 LM. The two lines insist more on the temporal aspect of development than on the opposition god/man, which as it were is marginalized by the indeterminacy of the personal pronoun "they" (see Babut [1977] 1994; cf. Fränkel 1975, 333).

39. *Sophistic Refutations*, 33.183b25–26.

40. See above, chap. 4, p. 108, n. 2.

CHAPTER 6: WHAT IS AT STAKE

1. See above, chap. 1, pp. 1–2.
2. Gadamer (1996) 2001. Aside from these lectures, most of the texts Gadamer dedicated to the Presocratics are to be found in the three volumes of his *Gesammelte Werke* (*GW*) that collect his writings on Greek philosophy (Gadamer 1985–1990).
3. *Sophist* 241d.
4. The whole of Parmenides's prologue and most of the first part (the truth of being) are preserved, together with the transition to the second part (cosmological opinions). The remains of this latter are scant, but the doxographical reports give us a fairly precise idea about it. The whole poem probably did not exceed the length of a short book of a Homeric epic, at most three hundred lines.
5. Gadamer (1996) 2001, 17.
6. Gadamer (1996) 2001, 15.
7. This is the first section of vol. 7 of his *Gesammelte Werke*.
8. See Heidegger 1979 (= GA 55), 41–42.
9. Reinhardt 1916, 66. Parmenides Fragment 28B6.4ff DK (= PARM. D7.4ff. LM) says, "this one [i.e. road of investigation], which mortals who know nothing / Invent [or: where mortals ... wander], two-headed [scil. creatures]! For the helplessness in their / Breast directs their wandering thought; and they are borne along, / Deaf and likewise blind, stupefied, tribes undecided [or: without judgment], / Who suppose that 'this is and is not' [or: that to be and not to be] is the same / And not the same ..."
10. On Zeller's relation to Hegel, cf. Laks 1999, 468–469; 2007, 17–18; cf. also above, chap. 2, pp. 20–21.
11. Gadamer 1985 (*GW*, vol. 6), 59.
12. The same tension can be found in Gadamer's interpretation of the relation between Aristotle and Plato, who often disagree but in the end always say the same thing.
13. Nietzsche, *Human All Too Human*, §261 ("The Tyrants of the Spirit") / Nietzsche 1980, 2:215.
14. This phenomenological interpretation, which goes along with a reevaluation of the relation between the two parts of Parmenides's poem, is based largely on the semantics of the term *noein*, which is often translated by "to think" but in fact designates a direct grasp, what Aristotle calls a "contact" (cf. Gadamer [1996] 2001, 103). For further references concerning the phenomenological reception of Parmenides, see the second part of Laks 2004b.

15. Gadamer 1985 (GW, vol. 6), 34. The quotations could be multiplied, see for example ibid., 59–60.

16. Plato, *Theaetetus* 179e.

17. Gadamer 1985 (GW, vol. 6), 60.

18. Ibid.

19. Hegel 1995, 166–167.

20. Cf. the quotation given above, p. 82. In Gadamer's "Heraklit-Studien," he calls Hegel the "great Aristotelian of modern times." Gadamer 1990 (GW, vol. 7), 82.

21. This term is usually translated as "reception history," though this English term does not render well the first part of the German compound, which means "effect" or "efficacy."

22. Gadamer (1996) 2001, 94.

23. In general, Gadamer's references to Cassirer are rare and not very significant.

24. Cassirer 1906, 20–50.

25. On the Neokantian interpretation of the Platonic theory of Ideas, see Laks 2004c. Natorp too was interested in the Presocratics: see especially his *Forschungen zur Geschichte des Erkenntnisproblems im Altertum* (1884), of which the title anticipates that of Cassirer's great later study.

26. On the significance of Cassirer's suppression of this chapter, see Krois 1996.

27. These intoductory lectures, to which I had access thanks to John Michael Krois, coeditor of Cassirer's *Nachlass*, do not present any major interest and are not included in the edition of Cassirer's *Nachgelassene Manuskripte und Texte* (Cassirer 1995–2014).

28. The chapter, dedicated to the history of ancient philosophy from Aristotle to the end of Antiquity, was written by Ernst Hoffmann ("Die antike Philosophie von Aristoteles bis zum Ausgang des Altertums"). The fact that this text was intended as an introductory manual is doubtless one reason it is read less widely than other writings of Cassirer are.

29. Burnet 1914.

30. On the extraordinary popularity of the Presocratics in the post-war period and their cultural significance, see Most 1995.

31. See above, chap. 2, p. 30.

32. Cassirer 1925, 85. On the connection thus formed between Plato and a philosophy of symbolic forms, cf. 89–90. On Cassirer's Plato, see Rudolph 2003.

33. Cassirer 1925, 11. The three stages correspond to physics (represented by its conclusion, Democritus), ethics (Socrates), and logic (the Platonic dialectic).

34. Cassirer 1925, 37.

35. Cassirer 1925, 18–19.

36. Cassirer 1925, 12.

37. Cassirer 1925, 23, with the opposition between "the hollows and crests of the wave" (*Wellenberge/-täler*) and "the form of the wave" (*die Form der Welle*).

38. Cassirer 1925, 26. Cf. above, chap. 1, p. 10.

39. Cassirer 1925, 28.

40. Cassirer 1925, 37.

41. Cassirer 1925, 37.

42. Cf. Parmenides, Fr. 8.29–30 = PARM. D8 34–35 LM.

43. Cassirer 1925, 45. This is the solution Cassirer proposes for what he considers "one of the most difficult questions of the whole history of philosophy."

44. "Nicht wieviel, sondern ob." Cassirer 1925, 39.

45. This theme is common to Cassirer and to Gadamer, except that the former distinguishes and articulates while the latter assimilates.

46. Parmenides Fr. 28B3 DK = D6.8 LM.

47. "And yet it is the most important achievement of Eleatic thought, and the genuinely decisive one, not only that it dialectically destroys the fundamental concepts of science but also that precisely in this destruction it creates the precondition for a new logical *determination* of these concepts." Cassirer 1925, 50.

48. Cassirer 1925, 50. There is a question whether one can qualify this physiology as "traditional," as Cassirer does—the idea of a harmony between *logos* and *phusis* being itself the result of the situation created by Parmenides. The question is that of the distance between the explicit and the implicit.

49. *Generation and Corruption* 1.8 324b35–325a28.

50. Cassirer 1925, 59.

51. Cassirer 1925, 56.

52. Comparison with Hegel is instructive here. For him, Anaxagoras represents an effective advance within Greek philosophy, however weak it might be, since "Understanding [*Verstand*] is recognized as the principle" (Hegel 1995, 319). By contrast, Empedocles is considered to be uninteresting ("much cannot be made of his philosophy"; ibid., 313).

53. Cassirer 1925, 63.

54. Cassirer 1925, 63.
55. Democritus Fr. 68B11 DK = D20 LM.
56. Cassirer 1925, 17.
57. Cassirer 1925, 8, 9, 10.
58. Cassirer 1925, 8. See on this point Cassirer 1932. The conviction according to which the history of philosophy is inseparable from the history of the sciences is part of his Kantian heritage.
59. Cassirer 1925, 16, 20, and 10 respectively.
60. Cassirer 1906, 18. The criticism returns in 1925, 12, where, against Zeller and Joël, Cassirer defends the idea of a philosophical history of philosophy that systematically sets aside the biographical and contextual data, whatever the charm and interest these might be granted.
61. Cassirer (1906) 1922, 19.
62. Cassirer (1906) 1922, 18.
63. Cassirer 1944, 228.
64. Cassirer 1925, 38.
65. Cassirer 1925, 40.
66. Cassirer 1925, 8–9.
67. On the problem of the relation between Cassirer and Hegel, see Ferrari 1990, 168–169.
68. Cassirer 1941, 4.
69. Cassirer 1925, 7.
70. Cassirer 1925, 8. "Pure" does not mean that the movement is not historical, but that the determinations of thought are considered for themselves, independently.
71. A fine illustration of this dialectic between image and concept in the case of a modern sequence can be found in Cassirer's analysis of the relation Kepler/Leibniz in *Freiheit und Form* (Cassirer 1917), where his ambition is to show in what regard the history of European, and more particularly of German, philosophy has a universal value, to the very extent to which through its successive forms it provides evidence of the progress of liberty. Recki (1997, 62) insists on the political dimension of this book, written in the midst of the First World War: Cassirer sets himself in opposition to the "polarization between profound German culture and superficial Western civilization … by demonstrating the continuity, in terms of the history of the spirit, of German, Italian, and French thought since the Renaissance."
72. Habermas 1997, 94 and 95.

BIBLIOGRAPHY

I. Modern Works and Studies

Assmann, A. 1989. "Jaspers' Achsenzeit, oder Schwierigkeiten mit der Zentralperspektive in der Geschichte." In *Karl Jaspers: Denken zwischen Wissenschaft, Politik und Philosophie*, edited by D. Harth, 187–205. Stuttgart.

Babut, D. (1977) 1994. "L'idée de progrès et la relativité du savoir humain chez Xénophane." *Revue de Philologie* 51: 217–28. Reprinted with the same pagination in D. Babut, *Parerga*. Lyon.

———. 1978. "Anaxagore jugé par Socrate et Platon." *Revue des études grecques* 91: 44–76.

Baur, F. Chr. 1876. *Drei Abhandlungen zur Geschichte der alten Philosophie und ihres Verhältnisses zum Christentum*. Leipzig.

Bernal, M. 1987. *The Fabrication of Ancient Greece*. Vol. 1 of *Black Athena: The Afroasiatic Roots of Classical Civilization*. London.

———. 1991. *The Archeological and Documentary Evidence*. Vol. 2 of *Black Athena: The Afroasiatic Roots of Classical Civilization*. London.

Betegh, G. 2004. *The Derveni Papyrus / Cosmology, Theology and Interpretation*. Cambridge.

———. 2013. "Socrate et Archélaos dans les *Nuées*. Philosophie naturelle et éthique." In *Comédie et Philosophie. Socrate et les 'Présocratiques' dans les Nuées d'Aristophane*, edited by A. Laks and R. Saetta-Cottone, 87–106. Paris.

Blackwell, C. 1997. "*Thales Philosophus*. The Beginning of Philosophy as a Discipline." In *History and the Disciplines: The Reclassification of Knowledge in Early Modern Europe*, edited by D. R. Kelley, 61–82. Rochester.

Bloom, H. 1987. *The Strong Light of the Canonical. Kafka, Freud and Scholem as Revisionists of Jewish Culture and Thought*. New York.

Blumenberg, H. (1966) 1983. *Die Legitimität der Neuzeit*. Frankfurt am Main. Translated by Robert M. Wallace as *The Legitimacy of the Modern Age*. Cambridge, MA.

Bollack, J. (1985) 2016. "Le modèle scientiste: Empédocle chez Freud." In *La Grèce de personne*, 107–114. Paris. Translated by Catherine Porter and Susan Tarrow, with Bruce King as "The Scientistic Model: Freud and Empedocles." In *The Art of Reading: From Homer to Paul Celan*, edited by Christoph Koenig, Leonard Muellner, Gregory Nagy, and Sheldon Pollock, 249–256. Washington, DC.

Borsche, T. 1985. "Nietzsches Erfindung der Vorsokratiker." In *Nietzsche und die philosophische Tradition*, edited by J. Simon, 62–87. Würzburg.

Buisine, A. 2002. *Les Sept Sages de la Grèce antique*. Paris.

Burckhardt, J. 1868. *Geschichte der Renaissance in Italien*. Stuttgart.

———. (1898/1902) 1977. *Griechische Kulturgeschichte*. 4 vols. Reprint, Munich.

Burkert, W. 1960. "Plato oder Pythagoras. Zum Ursprung des Wortes Philosophie." *Hermes* 88: 159–177.

———. (1962) 1972. *Lore and Science in Ancient Pythagoreanism*. Cambridge, MA.

———. 1970. "La genèse des choses et des mots. Le papyrus de Derveni entre Anaxagore et Cratyle." In *Les Études philosophiques* 25: 443–455.

———. 1979. "Mythisches Denken. Versuch einer Definition anhand des griechischen Befundes." In *Philosophie und Mythos. Ein Kolloquium*, edited by H. Poser, 16–39. Berlin.

———. 1992. *The Orientalizing Revolution: Near Eastern Influence on Greek Culture in the Early Archaic Age*. Cambridge, MA.

———. (1994–1995) 2003. "Orientalische und Griechische Weltmodelle von Assur bis Anaximandros." *Wiener Studien* 107/108: 179–186. Reprinted in W. Burkert, *Kleine Schriften*, vol. 2, *Orientalia*, edited by L. Gemelli Marciano, 223–229. Göttingen.

———. 2004. *Babylon, Memphis, Persepolis: Eastern Contexts of Greek Culture*. Cambridge, MA.

Burnet, J. 1892. *Early Greek Philosophy*. London.

———. 1914. *Greek Philosophy: Thales to Plato*. London.

Burnyeat, M. 1998. "*Dissoi Logoi*." In *The Routledge Encyclopedia of Philosophy*, edited by E. Craig, vol. 3, 106–107. London.

Buxton, R., ed. 1999. *From Myth to Reason? Studies in the Development of Greek Thought*. Oxford.

Calame, C. (1991) 2008. "'Mythe' et 'rite' en Grèce: des catégories indigènes?" *Kernos* 4:179–204. Reprinted in C. Calame, *Sentiers transverseaux*, 43–62. Grenoble.

Cambiano, G. 1988. *Il ritorno degli Antichi*. Rome.

Canfora, L. 1992. "Clemente di Alessandria e Diogene Laerzio." In *Storia poesia e pensiero nel mondo antico. Studi in onore di Marcello Gigante*, 79–81. Naples.

Cassirer, E. (1906) 1922. *Das Erkenntnisproblem in der Philosophie und Wissenschaft der neueren Zeit*. Vol.1. Berlin.

———. 1910. *Substanzbegriff und Funktionsbegriff: Untersuchungen über die Grundfragen der Erkenntniskritik*. Berlin.

———. 1917. *Freiheit und Form. Studien zur deutschen Geistesgeschichte*. Berlin.

———. (1922) 1969. "Die Begriffsform im mythischen Denken." In *Wesen und Wirkung des Symbolbegriffs*, 1–70. Darmstadt.

———. 1925. "Die Philosophie der Griechen von den Anfängen bis Platon." In *Lehrbuch der Philosophie*, vol. 1, *Die Geschichte der Philosophie*, edited by Max Dessoir, 7–139. Berlin.

———. 1932. "Die Entstehung der exakten Wissenschaften." *Die Antike* 8: 276–300.

———. (1935) 1979. "The Concept of Philosophy as a Philosophical Problem." In *Symbol, Myth, and Culture: Essays and Lectures of Ernst Cassirer 1935–1945*, edited by D. P. Verene, 49–63. New Haven, CT.

———. 1941. "*Logos, Dike, Kosmos*." *Acta Universitatis Gotoburgensis* 47 (6): 3–31.

———. 1944. *An Essay on Man. An Introduction to a Philosophy of Human Culture*. New Haven, CT.

———. 1946. *The Myth of the State*. New Haven, CT.

———. 1995–2014. *Nachgelassene Manuskripte und Texte*. 18 vols. Edited by K.C. Köhnke, J.-M. Krois, and O. Schwemmer. Hamburg.

Cherniss, H. (1935) 1964. *Aristotle's Criticism of Presocratic Philosophy*. Baltimore. Reprint, New York.

Cornford, F. M. 1912. *From Religion to Philosophy: A Study in the Origins of Western Speculation*. London.

———. 1952. *Principium sapientiæ. The Origins of Greek Philosophical Thought*. Cambridge.

Courtine, J.-F. 1999. "The Destruction of Logic: From Logos to Language." In *The Presocratics after Heidegger*, edited by D. C. Jacobs, 25–53. New York.

Detienne, M. (1981) 1986. *L'Invention de la mythologie*. Paris. Translated as *The Creation of Mythology* by Margaret Cook. Chicago. Citations refer to the translation.

Detienne, M., and Vernant, J.-P. (1974) 1991. *Les Ruses de l'intelligence. La Metis des Grecs*.Paris. Translated as *Cunning Intelligence in Greek Culture and Society* by Janet Lloyd. Chicago.

Diels, H. (1881) 1969. "Über Leukipp und Demokrit." In H. Diels, *Kleine Schriften zur Geschichte der antiken Philosophie*, edited by W. Burkert, 85–198. Darmstadt.

———. 1903. *Die Fragmente der Vorsokratiker*. Berlin.

Diels, H., and W. Kranz. 1951–1952. *Die Fragmente der Vorsokratiker*. 6th ed. revised by W. Kranz. Berlin.

Diller, H. (1946) 1966. "Hesiod und die Anfänge der giechischen Philoso-
    phie." *Antike und Abendland* 2: 140–151. Reprinted in *Hesiod*, edited
    by E. Heitsch, 688–707. Wege der Forschung 44. Darmstadt.

Donato, R. di. 1983. Postface to L. Gernet, *Les Grecs sans miracle, Textes
    1903–1960*, 493–420. Paris.

Eberhard, J. A. (1788) 1796. *Allgemeine Geschichte der Philosophie*. Halle.

Elkana, Y. 1986. "Second-Order Thinking in Classical Greece." In *Origins
    and Diversity of Axial Age Civilizations*, edited by S. N. Eisenstadt, 40–
    64. New York.

Ernesti, J. A. (1754) 1995. "*De philosophia populari*." French translation
    by R. Mortier. In *Popularité de la philosophie*, edited by Ph. Beck and
    D. Thouard, 371–379. Fontenay/Saint-Cloud.

Fascher, E. 1959. *Sokrates und Christus*. Leipzig.

Fazzo, S. 2009. "Diogene di Apollonia e le Nuvole di Aristofane: nota in-
    torno alle origini di un problema storiografico." *Aevum Antiquum* 8:
    161–168.

Ferrari, M. 1990. "La genèse de *Das Erkenntnisproblem*: le lien entre sys-
    tématique et histoire de la philosophie." In *Ernst Cassirer. De Marbourg
    à New York*, edited by J. Seidengart, 97–114. Paris.

Fränkel, H. 1975. *Early Greek Poetry and Philosophy*. Oxford.

Frede, M. 2004. "Aristotle's Account of the Origins of Philosophy." *Rhizai*
    1: 9–44.

Freud, S. (1937) 1964. "Analysis Terminable and Interminable." In *The
    Standard Edition of the Complete Psychological Works of Sigmund Freud*,
    vol. 23, *1937–1939*, 216–225. Translated from the German under the
    General Editorship of James Strachey. London.

Gadamer, H.-G. 1985. *Gesammelte Werke*. Vol. 5, *Griechische Philosophie, I.*
    Tübingen.

———. 1985. *Gesammelte Werke*. Vol. 6, *Griechische Philosophie, II.*
    Tübingen.

———. 1991. *Gesammelte Werke*. Vol. 7, *Griechische Philosophie, III.*
    Tübingen.

———. (1996) 2001. *Der Anfang der Philosophie*. Stuttgart. Translated as
    The Beginning of Philosophy by Rod Coltman. New York.

Gernet, L. (1945) 1968. *Les origines de la philosophie*. Plaquette. Rabat.
    Reprinted in *Anthropologie de la Grèce antique*, 415–30. Paris.

———. (1956) 1968. "Choses visibles et choses invisibles." *Revue
    Philosophique de la France et de l'Étranger* 146: 79–86. Reprinted in *An-
    thropologie de la Grèce antique*, 405–414. Paris.

———. 1968. *Anthropologie de la Grèce antique*. Paris.

———. (1945) 1983. Review of *Essai sur la formation de la pensée grecque*, by P. M. Schuhl, *Bulletin de l'enseignement public au Maroc* 183: 1–12. Reprinted in *Les Grecs sans miracle, Textes 1903–1960*, 212–222. Paris.

———. 1983. *Les Grecs sans miracle, Textes 1903–1960*. Paris.

Gigon, O. 1945. *Der Ursprung der griechischen Philosophie*. Basel.

Gorman, V. B. 2001. *Miletos, The Ornament of Ionia: A History of the City to 400 B.C.E.* Ann Arbor.

Gottschalk, H. B. 1980. *Heraclides of Pontus*. Oxford.

Habermas, J. (1981) 1987. *Theorie des kommunikativen Handelns*. Frankfurt am Main. Translated as *The Theory of Communicative Action* by T. McCarthy. 2 vols. Boston.

———. 1997. "Die befreiende Kraft der symbolischen Formgebung." In *Ernst Cassirers Werk und Wirkung. Kultur und Philosophie*, edited by D. Frede and B. Recki, 79–104. Darmstadt.

Hadot, I. 1987. "La vie et l'œuvre de Simplicius d'après des sources grecques et arabes." In *Simplicius, Sa vie, son œuvre, sa survie*, edited by I. Hadot, 3–39. Berlin.

Havelock, E. A. 1996. *Alle origini della filosofia greca: una revisione storica*. Edited by Th. Cole, translated by Liana Lomiento. Rome.

Hegel, G. W. F. 1995. *Lectures on the History of Philosophy*. 3 vols. Translated by E. S. Haldane and F. H. Simson, with introduction by F. C. Beiser. Lincoln. (This translation first published 1892–1896 is of the second edition of Hegel's *Vorlesungen über die Geschichte der Philosophie*, in 3 vols., edited by Karl Ludwig Michelet. Berlin, 1840–1844.)

Heidegger, M. 1979. *Heraklit* (= *Gesamtausgabe* 55). Frankfurt am Main.

———. 1982. *Parmenides* (= *Gesamtausgabe* 54). Frankfurt am Main.

Heuss, A. 1946. "Die archaische Zeit Griechenlands als geschichtliche Epoche." *Antike und Abendland* 2: 26–62.

Hölscher, U. 1968. *Anfängliches Fragen. Studien zur frühen griechischen Philosophie*. Göttingen.

Hoffmann, E. 1947. *Die Sprache und die archaische Logik*. Tübingen.

Humphreys, S. C. 1978. "The Work of Louis Gernet." In *Anthropology and the Greeks*, 76–106. London.

———. (1986) 2004. "Dynamics of the Greek 'Breakthrough': The Dialogue between Philosophy and Religion." In *The Strangeness of Gods: Historical Perspectives on the Interpretation of Athenian Religion*, 51–76. Oxford.

———. 1996. "From Riddle to Rigour. Satisfactions of Scientific Prose in Ancient Greece." In *Proof and Persuasion: Essays on Authority, Objectivity and Evidence*, edited by S. Marchand and E. Lunbeck, 3–24. Turnhout.

Idel, M. 2001. "On Binary 'Beginnings' in Kabbalah-Scholarship." In *Historicization/Historisierung*, edited by G.W. Most, 313–337. Göttingen.

Janz, C. P. 1974. "Friedrich Nietzsches *akademische* Lehrtätigkeit in Basel 1869–1879." *Nietzsche Studien* 3: 192–203.

Jaspers, K. (1949) 1953. *Vom Ursprung und Ziel der Geschichte*. Munich. Translated as *The Origin and Goal of History* by M. Bullock. London.

Jouan, F., and H. Van Looy. 2002. *Euripide, Tragédies. Fragments: De Aigeus à Autolykos*. Paris.

Jouanna, J., ed. 1990. *Hippocrate, L'Ancienne Médecine*. Paris.

Kahn, C. (1960) 1994. *Anaximander and the Origins of Greek Cosmology*. Cambridge, MA.

Kambitsis, J. 1972. *L'Antiope d'Euripide*. Athens.

Karsten, S. 1830, 1835, 1838. *The Remains of the Works of the Ancient Greek Philosophers, Especially of Those Who Flourished before Plato* (*Philosophorum graecorum veterum praesertim qui ante Platonem floruerunt operum reliquiae*). Part 1: *Xenophanes* (1830), Brussel; Part 2: *Parmenides* (1835), Amsterdam; Part 3: *Empedocles* (1838), Amsterdam.

Kerferd, G. (1981) 1999. *The Sophistic Movement*. Cambridge.

Kingsley, P. 1992. "Ezechiel by the Grand Canal: Between Jewish and Babylonian Tradition." *Journal of the Royal Asiatic Society* 3 (2): 339–346.

———. 1995. *Ancient Philosophy, Mystery and Magic. Empedocles and Pythagorean Tradition*. Oxford.

———. (1999) 2001. *In the Dark Places of Wisdom*. Inverness, CA. Reprint, London.

———. 2003. *Reality*. Inverness, CA.

Kleingünther, A. 1933. *Prôtos Heuretes. Untersuchungen zur Geschichte einer Fragestellung* (=*Philologus, Supplementband* 26:1). Leipzig.

Krois, J.-M. 1996. "A Note about Philosophy and History: The Place of Cassirer's *Erkenntnisproblem*." *Science in Context* 9: 191–194.

Krug, W. T. (1815) 1827. *Geschichte der Philosophie alter Zeit*. 2nd ed. Leipzig.

Laks, A. 1999. "Histoire critique et doxographie. Pour une histoire de l'historiographie de la philosophie." In *Etudes philosophiques*, 465–477. Revised version in Laks 2007, 13–26.

———. 2001. "Ecriture, Prose, et les débuts de la philosophie ancienne." *Methodos* 1: 131–151. Revised version in Laks 2007, 167–179.

———. 2004a. "Aristote, l'allégorie et les débuts de la philosophie." In *L'Allégorie de l'Antiquité à la Renaissance*, edited by B. Pérez-Jean and P. Eichel-Lojkine, 211–220. Paris. Revised version in Laks 2007, 160–166.

———. 2004b. "Gadamer et les Présocratiques." In *Gadamer et les Grecs*, edited by J-C. Gens, P. Konto, and P. Rodrigo, 13–29. Paris.

———. 2004c. "Plato between Cohen and Natorp." In P. Natorp, *Plato's Theory of Ideas*, translated by V. Politis and J. Connolly, 453–483. Sankt Augustin.

———. 2006. "Jacob le Cynique : Philosophes et philosophie dans la *Griechische Kulturgeschichte*." In *Jacob Burckhardt und die Griechen*, edited by L. Burckhardt and H. Gercke, 325–335. Beiträge zu Jacob Burckhardt 6. Basel.

———. 2007. *Histoire, Doxographie, Vérité. Etudes sur Aristote, Théophraste et la philosophie présocratique*. Louvain-la-Neuve.

———. (1983) 2008a. *Diogène d'Apollonie. Edition, traduction et commentaire des fragments et témoignages*. Lille/Paris. 2nd ed. Sankt-Augustin.

———. 2008b. "Le génie du rapprochement et les limites de la similitude: à propos de l'Anaximandre de Vernant." *Agenda de la pensée contemporaine* 10: 113–127.

———. 2015. "Das Proömium des Diogenes Laertios: Eine Frage der intellektuellen Mittelmeergeographie." In *Ein pluriverses Universum. Zivilisationen und Religionen im antiken Mittelmeerau*, edited by R. Faber & A. Lichtenberger, 241–252. Paderborn.

———. 2017. "Presocratic Ethics." In *The Cambridge Companion to Ancient Ethics*, edited by C. Bobonich, 11–29. Cambridge.

———. 2017. "Peut-on *lire* de Prologue des *Vies des philosophes* illustres de Diogène Laërce?" In *For a Skeptical Peripatetic: Festschrift in Honour of John Glucker*, edited by Y. Z. Liebersohn, I. Ludlam, and A. Edelheit, 285–94. Sankt Augustin.

Laks, A., and G. W. Most. *Early Greek Philosophy*. Loeb Classical Library. 9 vols. Cambridge, MA, 2016.

Laks, A., and R. Saetta-Cottone, eds. 2013. *Comédie et Philosophie. Socrate et les 'Présocratiques' dans les Nuées d'Aristophane*. Paris.

Lefkowitz, M. 1996. *Not Out of Africa: How Afrocentrism Became an Excuse to Teach Myth as History*. New York.

Livingstone, A. 1986. *Mystical and Mythological Explanatory Works of Assyrian and Babylonian Scholars*. Oxford.

Lloyd, G. E. R. (1972) 1991. "The Social Background of Early Greek Philosophy and Science." In *Methods and Problems in Greek Science*, 121–140. Cambridge.

———. 1997. *Adversaries and Authorities*. Cambridge.

———. 2002. "Le pluralisme de la vie intellectuelle avant Platon." In *Qu'est-ce que la philosophie présocratique ? / What is Presocratic Philosophy?*, edited by A. Laks and C. Louguet, 39–54. Lille.

Long, A., ed. 1999. *The Cambridge Companion to Early Greek Philosophy*. Cambridge.

Mansfeld, J. 1979/1980. "The Chronology of Anaxagoras' Athenian Period and the Date of his Trial." *Mnemosyne* 32: 39–69 and 33: 17–95. Reprint in Mansfeld 1990, 264–306.

———. 1985. "Myth Science Philosophy, A Question of Origins." In *Hypatia. Festschrift Hazel E. Barnes*, edited by W. M. Calder III, U. K. Goldsmith, P. B. Kenevan, 45–65. Boulder, CO. Reprint in Mansfeld 1990, 1–21.

———. 1986. "Aristotle, Plato, and the Preplatonic Doxography and Chronography." In *Storiographia e dossografia nella filosofia antica*, edited by G. Cambiano, 1–59. Turin. Reprinted in Mansfeld 1990, 22–83.

———. 1990. *Studies in the Historiography of Greek Philosophy*. Assen-Maastricht.

———. 1994. "A Lost Manuscript of Empedocles' *Katharmoi*." *Mnemosyne* 47: 79–82.

Mansfeld, J., and O. Primavesi. 2011. *Die Vorsokratiker*. Stuttgart.

Martin, A., and O. Primavesi. 1999. *L'Empédocle de Strasbourg (P.Strasb.gr. Inv. 1665–1666)*. Berlin.

Martin, R. P. 1989. *The Language of Heroes: Speech and Performance in the Iliad*. Ithaca, NY.

Meier, C. (1980) 1990. *Die Entstehung des Politischen bei den Griechen*. Frankfurt am Main. Translated as *The Greek Discovery of Politics* by David McLintock. Cambridge, MA.

———. 1986. "The Emergence of an Autonomous Intelligence among the Greeks." In *The Origins and Diversity of Axial Age Civilizations*, edited by S. N. Eisenstadt, 66–91. New York.

Meyerson, I. (1948) 1987. "Discontinuités et cheminements autonomes dans l'histoire de l'esprit." In *Ecrits 1920–1983. Pour une psychologie historique*, 53–65. Paris.

Momigliano, A. 1975. *Alien Wisdom. The Limits of Hellenization*. Cambridge.

Most, G. W. 1989. "Zur Archäologie der Archaik." *Antike und Abendland* 35: 1–23.

———. 1995. "*Polemos pantôn patèr*. Die Vorsokratiker in der Forschung der zwanziger Jahre." In *Altertumswissenschaft in den 20er Jahren*, edited by H. Flashar, 87–114. Stuttgart.

———. 2002. "Heidegger's Greeks." *Arion* 10 (1): 83–98.

Mullach, F. W. A. (1860) 1867. *Fragmenta philosophorum graecorum, I: Poeseos philosophicae caeterorumque ante Socratem philosophorum quae supersunt. II: Pythagoreos, Sophistas, Cynicos et Chalcidii in Priorem Timaei platonici partem commentarios continens*. Paris.

Musil, R. (1930/1932) 1995. *The Man without Qualities*. Translated by Sophie Wilkins. New York.

Naddaf, G. 2005. *The Greek Concept of Nature*. Albany.

Nagy, G. 1979. *The Best of the Achaeans*. Baltimore.

Narcy, M. 1997. "Rendre à Socrate … ou à Démocrite? (Aristote, *Métaphysique* M4, 1078b17–31." In *Lezione Socratiche*, edited by G. Giannantoni and M. Narcy, 81–97. Naples.

Natorp, P. 1884. *Forschungen zur Geschichte des Erkenntnisproblems im Alterthum*. Berlin.

Nestle, W. 1940. *Vom Mythos zum Logos; die Selbstentfaltung des griechischen Denkens von Homer bis auf die Sophistik und Sokrates*. Stuttgart.

Nietzsche, F. (1873) 1980. *Die Philosophie im tragischen Zeitalter der Griechen*. In Nietzsche 1980, vol. 1, 801–872.

———. (1876) 1980. *Unzeitgemässe Betrachtungen, Viertes Stück: Richard Wagner in Bayreuth*. In Nietzsche 1980, vol. 1, 429–510.

———. (1888) 1980. *Götzen-Dämmerung*. In Nietzsche 1980, vol. 6, 55–62.

———. (1889) 1980. *Ecce Homo*. In Nietzsche 1980, vol. 6, 255–315.

———. 1980. *Sämtliche Werke. Kritische Studienausgabe in 15 Bänden*. Edited by G. Colli and M. Montinari. Munich.

———. 1995. *Die Vorplatonischen Philosophen*. In *Nietzsche Werke: Kritische Gesamtausgabe*. Founded by G. Colli and M. Montinari. Vol. II/4, *Vorlesungsauzeichnungern (WS 1871/72–WS 1874/75)*. Berlin.

———. 2006. *The Preplatonic Philosophers*. Translated by Greg Whitlock. Champaign, IL.

Nightingale, A. W. 1995. *Genres in Dialogue: Plato's Construct of Philosophy*. Cambridge.

———. 2004. *Spectacles of Truth in Classical Greek Philosophy. Theoria in Its Cultural Context*. Cambridge.

Oppermann, H. 1929. *Die Einheit der vorsophistischen Philosophie*. Bonn.

Owen, G. E. L. 1986. "Logic and Metaphysics in Some Earlier Works of Aristotle." In *Logic, Science and Dialectic: Collected Papers in Greek Philosophy*, 180–199. Ithaca, NY.

Panofsky, E. 1960. *Renaissance and Renascences in Western Art*. Stockholm.

Paquet, L., and Y. Lafrance. 1995. *Les Présocratiques (1450–1879)*. Vol. 3 (Supplément). Québec.

Piano, V. 2016. *Il papiro di Derveni tra religione e filosofia* (STCPF 18). Florence.

Pohlenz, M. 1918. "Das zwanzigste Kapitel von Hippokrates *De prisca medicina*." *Hermes* 53: 396–421.

Popper, K. (1958–1959) 1965. "Back to the Presocratics!" In *Conjectures and Refutations: The Growth of Scientific Knowledge*, 136–153. London.

Primavesi, O. 2002. "Lecteurs antiques et byzantins d'Empédocle. De Zénon à Tzétzès." In *Qu'est-ce que la philosophie présocratique ? / What is Presocratic Philosophy?*, edited by A. Laks and C. Louguet, 183–204. Lille.

Ramelli, I. 2004. "Diogene Laerzio e i Cristiani: conoscenza e polemica con Taziano e con Clemente Alessandrino." *Espacio, Tiempo y Forma*, 2nd ser., 15: 27–42.

Recki, B. 1997. "Kultur ohne Moral? Warum Ernst Cassirer trotz der Einsicht in den Primat der praktischen Vernunft keine Ethik schreiben konnte." In *Ernst Cassirers Werk und Wirkung. Kultur und Philosophie*, edited by D. Frede and B. Recki, 58–78. Darmstadt.

Reinhardt, K. (1916) 1977. *Parmenides und die Geschichte der griechischen Philosophie*. Bonn. Reprint, Frankfurt am Main.

Renan, E. (1863) 1875. *Histoire des Origines du Christianisme*. Vol. 1, *La Vie de Jésus*. Paris. Translated as *The History of the Origins of Christianity*, vol. 1, *Life of Jesus* by William G. Hutchinson. London.

———. 1878 "Vingt jours en Sicile." In *Mélanges d'histoire et de voyages*, 77–118. Paris.

———. 1883. *Souvenirs d'Enfance et de Jeunesse*. Paris. Translated as *Recollections of My Youth* by C. B. Pitman and revised by Madame. New York.

Riedweg, Ch. 2002. *Pythagoras. Leben, Lehre, Nachwirkung*. Munich.

Rudolph, E. 2003. "Logos oder Symbol? Cassirer über Goethes Platonismus." In *Ernst Cassirer im Kontext*, edited by E. Rudolph, 243–253. Tübingen.

Saïd, E. W. 1975. *Beginnings: Intention and Methods*. Baltimore.

Sassi, M.-M. 2007. "Ordre cosmique et *isonomia*: en repensant *Les Origines de la pensée grecque* de Jean-Pierre Vernant." *Philosophie antique* 7: 187–218.

Schiefsky, M. J. 2005. *Hippocrates 'On Ancient Medicine'. Translated with Introduction and Commentary*. Leiden.

Schlechta, K., and A. Anders. 1962. *Friedrich Nietzsche. Von den verborgenen Anfängen seines Philosophierens*. Stuttgart/Bad-Canstatt.

Schleiermacher, F. W. D. (1815) 1835. "Über den Werth des Sokrates als Philosophen." In *Abhandlungen der königlichen-preussischen Akademie der Wissenschaften*, 50–68 = *Sämtliche Werke* 3. Abt., Bd. 2, 287–308. Berlin.

Schluchter, W. 1979. "The Paradox of Rationalization: On the Relation of Ethics and World." In *Max Weber's Vision of History*, edited by G. Roth and W. Schluchter, 11–64. Berkeley.

———. 1988. *Religion und Lebensführung*. 2 vols. Frankfurt am Main.

Schmalzriedt, E. 1970. *Peri phuseôs. Zur Frühgeschichte der Buchtitel*. Munich.

Scholem, G. 1969. *On the Kabbalah and Its Symbolism.* New York.

Schopenhauer, A. (1850) 1974. "Fragments for the History of Philosophy." In *Parerga and Paralipomena,* translated by E. F. J. Payne, vol. 1, 31–136. Oxford and New York.

Schwartz, B. 1975. "The Age of Transcendance." *Daedalus* 104: 1–7.

Seaford, R. 2004. *Money and the Early Greek Mind: Homer, Philosophy, Tragedy.* Cambridge.

Spencer, H. (1862) 1908. *First Principles.* 6th ed. London.

Thraede, K. 1962. "Das Lob des Erfinders. Bemerkungen zur Analyse der Heuremata-Kataloge." *Rheinisches Museum* 105: 158–186.

Tyrell, W. B. 2012. "Biography." In *Brill's Companion to Sophocles,* edited by A. Markantonatos, 19–38. Leiden and Boston.

Vander Waerdt, P. A. 1994. "Socrates in the Clouds." In *The Socratic Movement,* edited by Paul A. Vander Waerdt, 48–86. Ithaca, NY.

Vegetti, M. 1996. "Iatromantis." In *I signori della memoria e dell'oblio,* edited by M. Bettini, 65–81. Florence.

———. 1998. "Empedocle, Medico e sofista (*Antica Medicina* 20)." In *Text and Tradition. Studies in Ancient Medicine and Its Transmission. Presented to Jutta Kollesch,* edited by K. D. Fischer, D. Nickel, and P. Potter, 289–299. Leiden.

Vernant, J.-P. (1957) 2006. "The Formation of Positivist Thought in Archaic Greece." In *Myth and Thought among the Greeks,* translated by Janet Lloyd with Jeff Fort, 371–398. New York.

———. (1962) 1982. *Les Origines de la pensée Grecque,* Paris. Translated as *The Origins of Greek Thought.* Ithaca, NY.

———. (1975) 1996. "Questions de méthode. Dialogue avec Maurice Caveing et Maurice Godelier." In *Entre mythe et politique,* 105–136. Paris.

———. 1995. *Passé et Présent. Contributions à une psychologie historique.* 2 vols. Edited by R. di Donato. Rome.

———. 2007. *Œuvres. Religions, Rationalités, Politique.* 2 vols. Paris.

Weber, M. 1989. *Die Wirtschaftethik der Weltreligionen: Schriften 1915–1920.* Edited by H. Schmidt-Glintzer in collaboration with P. Kolonko. In *Max Weber Gesamtausgabe,* edited by H. Baier, M. R. Lepsius, W. J. Mommsen, W. Schluchter, and J. Winckelmann, Abteilung 1, Band 19, 31–522. Tübingen. (Partial translations: 1. *Introduction to the Economic Ethics of the World Religions.* In *The Essential Weber,* edited by Sam Whimster, 55–80. London, 2004. 2. *The Religion of China: Confucianism and Taoism.* Translated by H. H. Gerth. Glencoe, IL, 1951.)

———. 2016. *Die protestantische Ethik und der Geist des Kapitalismus.* Edited by W. Schulter and U. Bube. In Max Weber, *Gesamtausgabe,* edited by H. Baier, M. R. Lepsius, W. J. Mommsen, W. Schluchter, and J. Winckelmann, Abt. 1, Bd. 18, 101–492. Tübingen. Translated as *The Protestant Ethic and the Spirit of Capitalism* by T. Parsons. New York, 1958.

Weil, E. 1975. "What Is a Breakthrough in History?" *Daedalus* 104: 21–36.

West, M. L. (1966) 1978. *Hesiod. Theogony. Edited with Prolegomena and Commentary.* Oxford.

Wiese, H. 1963. "Heraklit bei Klemens von Alexandria." PhD diss., Kiel.

Windelband, W. 1891. *Geschichte der Philosophie.* Tübingen.

Zarader, M. 1986. *Heidegger et les paroles de l'origine.* Paris.

Zeller, E. (1844/1852) 1919/1923. *Die Philosophie der Griechen in ihrer geschichtlichen Entwicklung.* Edited by W. Nestle. 3 parts in 6 vols. Leipzig.

Zhmud, L. 2006. *The Origin of the History of Science in Classical Antiquity.* Berlin.

Zhmud, L., and A. Kouprianov, A. Forthcoming. "Ancient Greek *mathêmata* from a Sociological Perspective: A Quantitative Analysis." *Isis.*

2. Translations and Editions of Ancient Sources. Reference Works

Early Greek Philosophers

References to the fragments of the Presocratic authors are made, whenever possible, both to the edition of reference (Hermann Diels and Walter Kranz, *Die Fragmente der Vorsokratiker*, 6th edition, Berlin, 1951–1952, indicated as DK) and to the edition recently coedited by Glenn W. Most and myself (André Laks and Glenn W. Most, *Early Greek Philosophy*, Loeb Classical Library, 9 vols., Cambridge, MA, 2016, indicated as LM).

For Diogenes of Apollonia, see also:

Diogenes of Apollonia. In A. Laks (1983) 2008a. *Diogène d'Apollonie. Edition, traduction et commentaire des fragments et témoignages.* Lille/Paris. 2nd ed. Sankt-Augustin.

Other Authors

The titles of Plato's dialogues and Aristotle's individual works are not named separately in this bibliography.

Aristophanes. *Clouds.* In Aristophanes, *Clouds. Wasps. Peace*, edited and translated by J. Henderson. The Loeb Classical Library. Cambridge, MA, 1998.

Aristotle. *The Complete Works*. The revised Oxford translation. Edited by J. Barnes. Princeton, NJ, 1964.

Aristoteles. *Fragmenta selecta*. Edited by W. D. Ross. Oxford, 1955.

Cicero. *Tusculan Disputations*. With an English translation by J. E. King. The Loeb Classical Library. Cambridge, MA, 1971.

Diogenes Laertius. *Lives of Eminent Philosophers*. With an English translation by R. D. Hicks. The Loeb Classical Library. 2 vols. Cambridge, MA, 1925.

Doxographi Graeci. Edited by H. Diels. Berlin, 1876.

Epicurus. *Letter to Pythocles*. In B. Inwood and L. P. Gerson, *Hellenistic Philosophy: Introductory Readings*, 19–28. Indianapolis, 1997.

Eudemus. *Eudemos von Rhodos*. In *Die Schule des Aristoteles*, vol. 8, edited by F. Wehrli. Basel, 1969.

Eudemus of Rhodes. Edited by I. Bodnár and W. W. Fortenbaugh (RUSH XI). New Brunswick, NJ, 2002.

Euripides. *Fragments*. In *Euripides*, vol. 7 (Aegeus-Meleager), edited and translated by Ch. Collard and M. Cropp. The Loeb Classical Library. Cambridge, MA, 2008.

Heraclidus Ponticus. *Heracleides Pontikos*. In *Die Schule des Aristoteles*, vol. 7, edited by F. Wehrli. Basel, 1969.

Herodotus. *The Histories*. Translated by R. Waterfield. Oxford, 2008.

Hesiod. *Theogony*. Edited by M. L. West. Oxford, 1978.

Hesiod. *Theogony, Works and Days, Testimonia*. Edited and translated by G. W. Most. The Loeb Classical Library. Cambridge, MA, 2006.

Hippocrates. *Ancient Medicine*. In M. J. Schiefsky, *Hippocrates "On Ancient Medicine." Translated with Introduction and Commentary*. Leiden, 2005.

———. *Fleshes*. In *Hippocrates*, vol. 8, edited and translated by P. Potter. The Loeb Classical Libray. Cambridge, MA, 1995.

Homer. *Odyssey*. Translated by R. Lattimore. New York, 1999.

Isocrates. *Antidosis*. In *Isocrates*, vol. 2, with an English translation by G. Norlin. The Loeb Classical Library. Cambridge, MA, 1929.

Menander. *Fragmenta*. In *Poetae Comici Graeci*, vol. 6/2, edited by R. Kassel and C. Austin. Berlin, 1998.

Plato. *Complete Works*. Edited by J. M. Cooper, associate editor D. S. Hutchinson. Indianapolis, 1997.

Sextus Empiricus. *Against the Physicists*. In Sextus Empiricus, *Against the Physicists. Against the Ethicists*. With an English translation by R. G. Bury. The Loeb Classical Library. Cambridge, Mass./London 1936.

Simplicius. *Commentary on Aristotle's Physics*. In Simplicius, *In Aristotelis Physica Commentaria*, edited by H. Diels. *Commentaria in Aristotelem Graeca*, vols. 9–10. Berlin, 1882–1885.

Theophrastus. *Opinions of the Philosophers (Physikôn doxai)*. In *Doxographi Graeci*, edited by H. Diels, 473–495. Berlin, 1876.

Theophrastus. *On Sensation*. In *Doxographi Graeci*, edited by H. Diels, 497–527. Berlin, 1876.

Thucydides. *History of the Peloponesian War*. Edited and translated by M. Hammond. Oxford, 2009.

Xenophon. *Memorabilia*. In *Memorabilia. Oeconomicus*. Edited and translated by E. C. Marchant. *Symposium. Apology*. Translated by O. J. Todd, revised by J. Henderson. The Loeb Classical Library. Cambridge, MA, 2013.

Reference Works

H. Bonitz. *Index Aristotelicus*. Berlin, 1870.

INDEX

w/ a special emphasis on Plato

intro to the world of ideas into which
X.ty entered the world.

CPSIA information can be obtained
at www.ICGtesting.com
Printed in the USA
BVHW031810230120
570334BV00001B/84